About this Book

The Nexus 9 is Google's latest tablet computer and has a faster processor, bigger screen, higher screen resolution and better cameras than its forerunner, the best selling Nexus 7. The Nexus 9 introduces Android 5 Lollipop, the latest version of the Android operating system. With a new, bright and colourful screen layout known as Material Design, the Lollipop operating system is proving very popular.

The material in this book is also applicable to Nexus 7 and Nexus 10 machines which have been upgraded to Android 5 Lollipop.

The first chapter compares the Nexus 9 with other types of computer and outlines its many applications such as news, entertainment, web browsing, e-mail and social networking. Setting up the Nexus 9 and connecting to the Internet is discussed, followed by the basic methods of operation and alternative input methods such as voice recognition. The Home and All Apps screens are discussed, together with installing and managing "apps" from the thousands available in the Play Store.

Features such as Google Cards, Google Now and Maps are described, including using the Nexus 9 as a Sat Nav. Browsing the Web using Google Chrome is discussed at length. eBooks, music, video and live and catchup TV are described, together with e-mail and social networks such as Facebook and Twitter.

Later chapters discuss the use of the cameras on the Nexus 9 and importing photos from other devices such as SD card readers and smartphones. Using Dropbox and Google Drive to store files in the "clouds" is then covered, together with the free Google Docs office software. "Syncing" files between computers via the clouds is also discussed, as well as using a PC computer to manage the files on a Nexus 9. Using Google Cloud Print to output Nexus 9 documents and photos is then explained.

The Appendix describes the connection of various peripheral devices to the Nexus 9, using an OTG cable and also Bluetooth.

About the Author

Jim Gatenby trained as a Chartered Mechanical Engineer and initially worked at Rolls-Royce Ltd., using computers in the analysis of jet engine performance. He obtained a Master of Philosophy degree in Mathematical Education by research at Loughborough University of Technology and taught mathematics and computing for many years to students of all ages and abilities, in school and in adult education.

The author has written over forty books in the fields of educational computing, Microsoft Windows and more recently, tablet computers. His most recent books have included "An Introduction to the Nexus 7" and "Android Tablets Explained For All Ages", both of which have been very well-received.

Trademarks

Google, Google Drive, Google Chrome, Chromecast, Gmail, Google Cloud Print and YouTube are trademarks or registered trademarks of Google, Inc. Microsoft Windows, Microsoft Word, Microsoft Publisher, Microsoft Excel and Skype are trademarks or registered trademarks of Microsoft Corporation. Facebook is a registered trade mark of Facebook, Inc. Twitter is a registered trademark of Twitter, Inc. Amazon Kindle is a trademark or registered trademark of Amazon.com, Inc. Dropbox is a trademark or registered trademark of Dropbox, Inc. All other brand and product names used in this book are recognized as trademarks or registered trademarks, of their respective companies.

Acknowledgements

I would like to thank my wife Jill for her support during the preparation of this book and also Michael Babani for making the project possible.

Please Note

Although every care has been taken with the production of this book to ensure that all information is correct at the time of writing and that any projects, designs, modifications and/or programs, etc., contained herewith, operate in a correct and safe manner and also that any components specified are normally available in Great Britain, the Publishers and Author do not accept responsibility in any way for the failure (including fault in design) of any project, design, modification or program to work correctly or to cause damage to any equipment that it may be connected to or used in conjunction with, or in respect of any other damage or injury that may be so caused, nor do the Publishers accept responsibility in any way for the failure to obtain specified components.

Notice is also given that if equipment that is still under warranty is modified in any way or used or connected with home-built equipment then that warranty may be void.

British Library Cataloguing in Publication Data:

A catalogue record for this book is available from the British Library

ISBN 978-0-85934-753-2

Cover Design by Gregor Arthur

Printed and bound in Great Britain for Bernard Babani (publishing) Ltd

An Introduction to the Nexus 9

Jim Gatenby

BERNARD BABANI (publishing) LTD
The Grampians
Shepherds Bush Road
London W6 7NF
England

www.babanibooks.com

521 526 36 1

Contents

3

Exploring the Nexus 9   23

4

Further Features   37

5

Entertainment   55

Essential Jargon

App

An application or program which a user runs, such as a game.

Operating System (O.S.)

The software used to control all aspects of the running of a computer. The Nexus 9 uses the *Android 5 Lollipop* O.S.

Processor

A chip executing millions of program instructions per second.

RAM (Random Access Memory)

The main memory, temporarily storing the current app.

Internal Storage

Permanent storage on which apps and files can be saved. The Nexus 9 uses an SSD (Solid State Drive) with no moving parts.

Cloud Computing

Saving files on large *server computers* on the Internet, leaving more space on the Internal Storage of your tablet computer.

Syncing

Automatically copying and updating your files to the clouds, i.e. the Internet, so they are accessible to other computers.

Online

Connected to the Internet.

Screen Resolution

The number of dots or *pixels* on the screen. The Nexus 9 has a resolution of 2048x1536, or about 287 dots per inch.

Streaming

This allows you to watch videos or listen to music *temporarily*, without saving a copy on your tablet's Internal Storage.

Downloading

A file is copied from the Internet and saved on your tablet. It can be accessed anytime in the future, even if you are offline.

Nexus 9: An Overview

The Tablet Phenomenon

Hand-held tablet computers such as the Google Nexus 9 and the Apple iPad now meet a lot of the computing needs of many people. The Nexus 9 can match the iPad in many respects and despite its tiny size in relation to laptop and desktop machines, the Nexus 9 has real computing power.

Apart from over a million *apps* for news, entertainment and searching for information, the Nexus 9 also includes free apps for creating, saving and managing documents in the "clouds" on the Internet. So later you don't need to worry about where to retrieve them from, as discussed later.

The Nexus 9 embraces the latest technology, such as *voice searching* which really works. An in-built *GPS* (*Global Positioning System*) allows the Nexus 9 to identify your current location, so that relevant information such as traffic news can be displayed. Together with *Google Maps*, GPS also allows the Nexus 9 to be used to plan routes and to act as a Sat Nav.

Google Nexus 9 showing the All Apps screen

The Power of the Nexus 9

Anyone could be forgiven for thinking that a hand-held tablet like the Nexus 9 could not be as powerful as the more traditional laptop and desktop computers. In fact, the Nexus 9 and its forerunner the Nexus 7 are more powerful than many of the large computers of a few years ago. This is confirmed by looking at the critical components which affect computer performance. These are the *processor*, (the "brains" of a computer) and the *memory* or *RAM*, used to temporarily store the current app. A *Solid State Drive (SSD)* is used as internal storage for permanently saving apps, photos and document files, etc. The following table compares the Nexus 9 with its predecessor, the Nexus 7.

	Nexus 9 (2014)	Nexus 7 (2013)
Android O.S. version	5 Lollipop	4 KitKat
Processor speed	1.7GHz	1.5GHz
Internal storage	16 or 32GB	16 or 32GB
Memory (RAM)	2GB	2GB
Screen resolution (pixels)	2048x1536	1920x1200
Screen size (diagonal)	8.9 inches	7.0 inches
Cameras	Front 1.6MP Rear 8MP	Front 1.2MP Rear 5MP
Battery life between charges	9 hrs 30mins	9 hrs

(Android 4 KitKat above can be upgraded to Android 5 Lollipop. Updates to the Lollipop O.S. are designated 5.0.1, 5.0.2, etc.)

Many laptop and desktop PCs have inferior processor speeds and less RAM than the Nexus 9. Laptop and desktop PCs typically have 500GB or 1TB (terabyte) of internal storage on a *hard disc drive*. The Nexus 9 uses *cloud storage* so doesn't need a large hard disc drive, as discussed on the next page.

How is it Possible?

How can a tiny hand-held tablet, roughly the size of this book, contain a powerful computer? After all, the tower units which contain the critical components for many desktop machines are often the size of a small suitcase. Here are some reasons:

Cloud Computing

The Nexus 9 has no bulky hard disc drive — just a small, compact SSD, as mentioned on the previous page. The Nexus 9 doesn't need a big hard disc drive because all your documents, etc., are automatically sent to the *clouds*. The clouds are *servers* or computer systems on the Internet with massive storage capacity. These include *Google Drive*, *Dropbox* and *Microsoft OneDrive*. Photos and documents etc., stored in the clouds, can be accessed from any Internet computer, anywhere.

Input and Output Ports

Laptop and desktop computers have lots of bulky ports, sockets and cables for connecting monitors, mice, keyboards and printers, etc. The Nexus 9 has only two tiny ports or sockets.

The Nexus 9 has an *on-screen keyboard* which pops up when needed. Tiny speakers, microphones and two cameras are built-in on the Nexus 9, so large ports are not needed. The Nexus 9 has a *micro USB* port into which devices such as a keyboard, mouse, SD card or flash drive can be connected. The Nexus 9 is powered by a very small battery. The desktop machine requires a *Power Supply Unit* as big as a half a shoebox.

Downloading Music, Video and Software

There is no CD or DVD drive on the Nexus 9, like those fitted to laptop and desktop computers. Early desktop machines also had *floppy disc drives*. Nowadays you can *download* and *stream* music, videos and software (apps) from the Internet to your computer — so you don't need a CD or DVD drive.

So the use of the "clouds" for storage has enabled the development of powerful hand-held devices like the Nexus 9.

Nexus 9 vs Laptops and Desktops

When tablets first became very popular a few years ago, some people thought this spelled the end for laptop and desktop computers. Tablets have certainly dented the sales of the bigger machines and replaced them completely in some situations.

It really depends on what you want to do with a computer. I use all three types of machine most days — tablet, laptop and desktop:

- To check the news, weather, look something up on Google, read a newspaper, send a short e-mail, listen to music or watch catchup TV, I reach for the Nexus 9.

- To write a long e-mail, work on a chapter of this book, fill in an order form online, etc., with freedom to work <u>in any room in the house</u>, I would use my laptop.

- For working on long documents I use my desktop machine, permanently installed in the home office, with a 22-inch screen, large keyboard and mouse and ample work surfaces for spreading out papers, etc.

For people who need to work <u>anywhere</u>, on the move, etc., the Nexus 9 is a good choice, being much more portable than a laptop. However, the Nexus 9 and other tablets are rather small for producing long documents. Also I find accurate typing using the on-screen keyboard quite difficult using the fingers but much easier using a cheap *stylus*. (Like a pen with a soft rubber tip.)

Using the Nexus 9 Like a Laptop

If you want to use the Nexus 9 like a laptop, you can buy a separate keyboard, which doubles up as a cover. As discussed later in this book, you can also buy inexpensive USB, wireless and Bluetooth keyboards and mice for the Nexus 9. The **Create** folder installed on the Nexus 9 from new includes word processing and other office software, as discussed later. Adaptors are available to connect a Nexus 9 to an HDMI television for watching videos, etc.

Typical Uses of the Nexus 9

- Reading the latest news and weather forecasts.
- Reading online editions of newspapers and magazines.
- Reading eBooks using Google Books or the Kindle app for Android tablets like the Nexus 9.
- Listening to music and watching videos.
- Watching live and catchup TV and radio.
- Importing, viewing and editing photographs.
- Searching the Web for information using Google and the Chrome web browser.
- Searching the Web using *Google Voice Search*.
- Using Google Maps and Google Earth.
- Using the Nexus 9 as a Sat Nav.
- Sending and receiving e-mails.
- Using social networks, such as Facebook and Twitter.
- Using the *Skype* Internet telephone service to make free, worldwide, voice and video calls.
- Buying goods from online retailers such as Amazon.
- Finding out about holidays and booking online, including checking in to flights online.
- Playing games such as Solitaire and Chess.
- Finding the answer to obscure crossword clues.
- Creating and editing text documents and small spreadsheets, including *speech recognition* text input.
- Tracking live flight information of aircraft including location, speeds, altitude, bearing and ETA.
- Tracking the delivery progress of items ordered online.
- Managing your online bank account and finances.

Keep Your Laptop or Desktop Computer?

As shown by the examples on the previous page, there's a huge range of activities possible with a tablet computer like the Nexus 9. However, there are some tasks for which you really need a laptop or desktop machine. The following tasks would be easier to accomplish on a desktop or laptop computer rather than on a tablet like the Nexus 9.

- Typing a long document such as a letter, CV, report or student dissertation.
- Desktop publishing, including text and graphics, such as producing and editing a pamphlet, magazine or typesetting a book such as this one.
- Creating and editing a large spreadsheet, balance sheet for a business, personal accounts or large tables of text and figures.
- On-line forms and questionnaires requiring precise selection from menus and multiple choice answers.
- Design work such as architecture, graphic design, maps or engineering drawings (CAD).
- Creating, editing and updating websites.
- Maintaining a large customer database.

As mentioned elsewhere, there are various ways to increase the productivity of the Nexus 9, such as connecting a separate keyboard and mouse. You can connect the Nexus 9 to a laptop or desktop PC, as discussed later in this book, then use the PC to manage the files on the Nexus 9.

Ideally, if you can afford it, you will probably want to keep your laptop or desktop machine if you need to carry out weightier tasks like those listed above.

The Android Operating System

The *operating system* is a suite of programs or instructions which control every aspect of the computer's running. This differs from *applications* or *apps*, which are programs designed for a specific task, such as reading an eBook, editing a photograph or writing and sending an e-mail. Regardless of what app you are currently running, the operating system is constantly working in the background, controlling such functions as the screen display, saving documents or printing on paper.

The Android operating system for the Nexus 9 is produced by Google and widely used on tablets and smartphones. At the time of writing, in 2015, *Android 5 Lollipop* is the latest version.

The Google Play Store

Over a million apps or programs have been developed to work with the Android operating system and these are available from the Google Play Store, either free or costing just a few pounds.

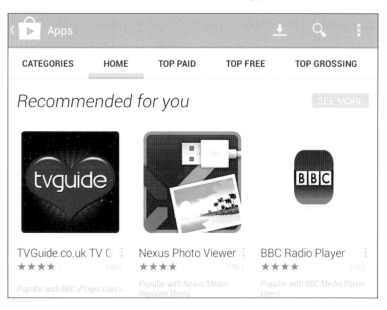

Apps are available for every conceivable purpose from games, music and entertainment, to health, fitness and lifestyle, for example.

Many apps are pre-installed on a new Nexus 9 and you can install additional apps from the Play Store. Your apps appear as icons on the Home screen and on the All Apps screen, as shown in the small sample below.

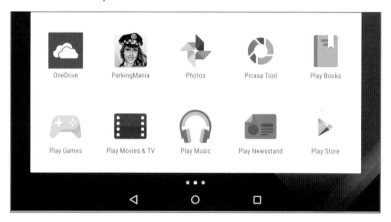

You can arrange groups of apps in folders representing different categories, such as Social Networking or Games, for example. The icons can be moved to new positions around the Home screen. These topics are discussed in more detail in Chapter 3.

Operating the Nexus 9

The Nexus 9 is mainly operated using touchscreen gestures, such as *tapping* and *swiping*. For example, to launch Google, simply use your finger to tap the Google icon shown on the next page. Instead of the finger you can tap the icons with an inexpensive *stylus*, similar to a pen with a rubber tip. Touchscreen gestures are discussed in more detail in Chapter 2. (To launch Google, you can also tap the microphone icon and say "**OK Google**" or swipe up from the bottom of the screen). *Voice searching* using spoken keywords is another option.

Some Favourite Apps

Apps appear as icons on the Home screen and the All Apps screen, as discussed in more detail in Chapter 3. An app is launched using a single tap on its icon, using a finger or a stylus. Listed below are some very popular and useful apps for the Nexus 9, together with their icons.

Play Store

The **Play Store** icon gives access to over a million apps in different categories. These are either free or can be bought online for a few pounds. When a new app is installed on your computer its icon appears on the Home and All Apps screens.

Google

Google is the world famous *search engine*. "To Google" means to search for information on a particular subject, after typing in some relevant *keywords.* The Nexus 9 can also use *voice recognition* for entering the keywords by speaking.

Chrome

Google Chrome is a *web browser*, similar to Microsoft's Internet Explorer and Apple's Safari. A web browser is used to display web pages and to move between pages using *links*. You can also revisit web pages from your *browsing history* or which you've *bookmarked* for future viewing.

Gmail

Google mail or **Gmail** is a free and popular e-mail service allowing you to send and receive messages consisting of text, pictures and attached files. Creating a Gmail account and password gives you access to several other Google services.

Earth

Google Earth allows you to zoom in and view different parts of the globe, using satellite images, aerial photography and images taken by cameras mounted on cars all over the world.

YouTube

YouTube is a free Google website which allows individuals and companies to upload and share videos for other people to view. These may include amusing incidents or popular music videos. If a video spreads quickly and is viewed by millions of people, it is said to "go viral".

Skype

Skype allows you to make free Internet telephone calls between computers. The Skype app is free and the Nexus 9 has the necessary built-in microphone, speakers and cameras. These enable free *video calls*, as well as voice calls, to be made to friends and family all over the world.

Facebook

Facebook is the leading *social networking* website. Users of Facebook post their *Profile* or *Timeline* on the Internet, allowing them to become online *friends* with people of similar interests. Friends exchange news, information, photographs and videos, etc. Businesses and celebrities can also use Facebook for publicity.

Twitter

Twitter is another very popular social networking website, on which users post short messages or *tweets* (up to 140 characters long). Some celebrities use Twitter to air their views and they may have thousands of followers. You can follow whoever you like, send replies to *tweets*, or use Twitter to enlist support for a campaign.

Amazon Kindle

The Nexus 9 has its own app, Google Books, for reading eBooks, but you can also download the free **Kindle** app, the software used on the original Kindle eBook reader from Amazon. There are millions of books, magazines and games available to download cheaply.

2

Setting Up the Nexus 9

Introduction

When you first take the Nexus 9 out of the box, you may be as surprised as I was that such a slender tablet, (also known as a *slate)*, can house a powerful computer. As discussed in Chapter 1, this is because a tablet doesn't need the bulky components like a hard drive, power supply unit, CD or DVD drive or large sockets to accommodate cables for peripheral devices. Thanks to technical advances such as *cloud computing*, based on the Internet, these large components, normally found in laptop and desktop computers, are not needed in tablets.

Charging the Battery

Apart from the Nexus 9 itself, the only other contents in the box are the battery charger plug and cable and a couple of flimsy leaflets. No assembly work is needed. Although the battery may be partially charged on delivery, you are advised to charge it fully before you get started. One end of the charging cable plugs into the *micro USB port* on the bottom of the tablet, as shown on the next page. The other end of the cable has a full-size USB connector which can be inserted into the 3-pin 13-amp charger plug provided. Alternatively the charging cable can be inserted into a USB port on a laptop or desktop computer. Charging using a computer should be carried out with the Nexus 9 in sleep mode or switched off. This method of charging is slower than when the Nexus 9 is connected to a charger plugged into a wall socket.

The battery life between charges is quoted as 9 hours 30 minutes, but varies depending on the type of activity.

Front Camera   Speaker   Headset socket   Rear Camera
1.6MP   8MP
                                           Flash LED
                                           Pinhole microphone
                                           Power/Lock key
                                           Volume key

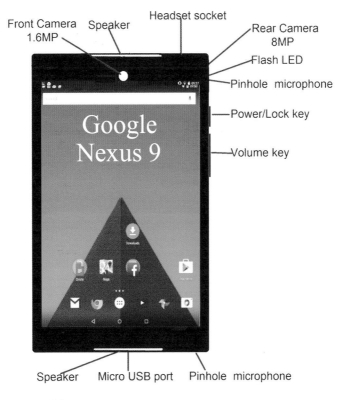

Speaker   Micro USB port   Pinhole microphone

Starting Up

Hold down the *Power/lock key*, shown above on the top right, until the word **Google** appears on the screen, followed by the *lock screen* as shown on the right. *Swipe* the padlock icon by touching it and sliding the finger across the screen. This opens the *Home screen*, discussed in the next chapter. Other methods of unlocking the Nexus 9 are discussed shortly.

Connecting to Wi-Fi

In the home, this often means connecting to a *broadband router*, usually included when you take out a contract with an Internet Service Provider such as BT, Virgin or Sky. Or it may mean connecting to the Wi-Fi network in a hotel or café, etc.

After selecting your language, the Nexus 9 should automatically detect any available Wi-Fi networks. Alternatively swipe down *twice* from the top of the screen to display the *Quick Settings* panel shown below.

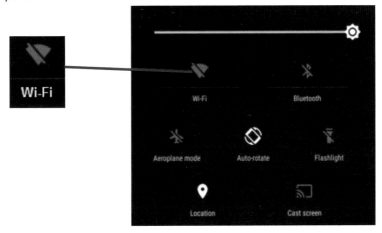

Now tap **Wi-Fi** or its icon shown above. If necessary, on the next screen to appear, tap the circle shown on the right and below to turn **Wi-Fi On**. This displays a list of available networks, as shown below.

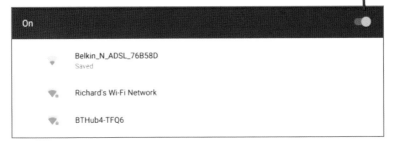

The small padlock icon shown on the right indicates a *secure network,* requiring a password to be entered before you can connect to it.

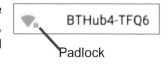

Padlock

Tap the name of the router or network you wish to connect to. The on-screen keyboard, shown on page 20, automatically pops up, enabling you to enter the password for the network, as shown below.

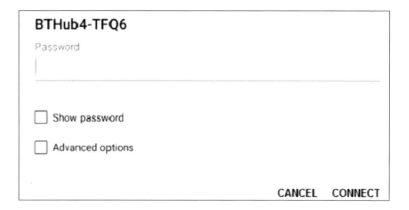

The name and password for a home network can usually be found on the back of the router. In an establishment such as a hotel or café, you may need to ask the staff for the password for their Wi-Fi. Some organisations now provide free Wi-Fi and you may not always need a password.

Tap **CONNECT** shown above to complete the process of getting online to the Internet. The word **Connected** should now appear next to the name of your selected router or Wi-Fi network, as shown below.

Checking Your Wi-Fi Connection

You can check your Wi-Fi settings at any time by swiping down _twice_ from the top of the screen to display the **Quick Settings** panel shown on page 13. Instead of "**Wi-Fi**", the panel should now display the name of your network, as shown in the extract on the right. The amount of white in the sector shown on the right and above indicates the strength of the Wi-Fi signal. Tapping the sector switches the Wi-Fi On and Off.

If you tap the name of your network, such as **BTHub4-TFQ6** in this example, the list of all of the nearby networks is displayed, as shown at the bottom of page 13. The word **Connected** should appear next to your network as shown at the bottom of page 14.

Tap your network's name in the list of available networks to see the **Status** of your connection, as well as the **Signal strength**, **Frequency**, type of **Security**, etc., as shown below.

BTHub4-TFQ6

Status
Connected

Signal strength
Excellent

Link speed
270Mbps

Frequency
5GHz

Security
WPA2 PSK

FORGET   FINISHED

Tap **FORGET** shown above to remove a redundant network from the list, such as a network you used while on holiday.

Creating a Gmail Account on the Nexus 9

If you haven't got a Gmail account with an e-mail address and password, you can create one during the initial setting up process for a new Nexus 9. It's worth opening a Gmail account because it gives access to several other free Google services, such as Google Drive cloud computing, as discussed in Chapters 1 and 9. Drive includes the Google Docs free office software.

You can create a new Google account at any time after swiping down twice from the top of the screen to open the **Quick Settings** panel. Then tap the **Settings** icon at the top of the panel, as shown on the right and in the extract below.

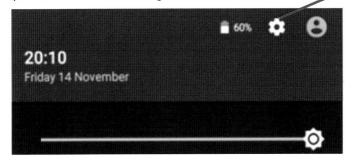

Another **Settings** icon, shown on the right, appears on the All Apps screen discussed in Chapter 3. Tapping either of the **Settings** icons opens the main **Settings** screen shown on page 47. Tap **Accounts** and then tap **+ Add account**. Then tap **Google** and **CREATE A NEW ACCOUNT**. Then enter your name and a suitable e-mail address and password, such as **jimsmith@gmail.com**. If the e-mail address has already been taken, add a few numbers to make it unique, such as **jimsmith99@gmail.com**.

Sharing Google Drive and Google Docs with a PC or Mac

With a Google account you can access Google Drive and Google Docs on your Nexus 9 and also on PC and Mac computers at:-

www.google.com

Rotation of the Screen

Swipe down twice from the top of the screen to open the **Quick Settings** panel shown on page 13. Tapping the icon in the centre of the panel changes the display between the **Portrait** and **Auto-Rotate** modes shown on the right.

In **Portrait** mode, the display is fixed for viewing with the tablet in the upright position, i.e. with the long sides vertical. In the **Auto-Rotate** setting, when you turn the Nexus 9 through 90 degrees, the screen display also rotates so that you can still read it.

Sleep Mode

If you don't use the Nexus 9 for a set period of time while it's switched on, the screen goes blank. This is the low power consumption *sleep mode*. You can also put the Nexus 9 into sleep mode by briefly pressing the Power/Lock button shown on page 12.

Sleep mode saves battery life and may also be necessary for security if you're going to leave the tablet unattended. When you wake the Nexus 9 up from sleep mode, you need to unlock it by swiping the padlock icon discussed on page 12 or using one of the other *unlocking* methods discussed on the next page.

Waking Up the Nexus 9 from Sleep

Tap the screen twice

Or: Press the Power/Lock key

Setting the Inactivity Time Before Sleep Mode is Entered

Tap the **Settings** icon shown on page 16 and select **Display** from the main **Settings** screen shown on page 47. Then tap **Sleep** and tap to select the required period of time from the list, which has options from 15 seconds to 20 minutes.

Locking and Unlocking the Screen

After you switch the Nexus 9 on by holding down the Power/Lock key, the screen is initially in the *locked* or inaccessible state. By default, a new Nexus 9 screen is unlocked by swiping away the padlock icon, as discussed on page 12. However, there are several alternative ways to unlock the screen, especially if you want to make the Nexus 9 more secure.

Open the main **Settings** screen shown on page 47 by tapping the **Settings** icon discussed on page 16. Now tap **Security** on the right of the screen. As shown on the right, the default method of unlocking the screen is to **Swipe** the padlock icon upwards.

Tap **Screen lock** shown above to see the list of alternative methods of unlocking the screen.

If your tablet holds important or sensitive data you may wish to secure it with a **PIN** number or **Password** as shown on the right. Alternatively you can create and save a unique **Pattern** by joining up a series of dots on the screen.

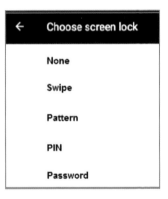

Shutting Down the Nexus 9

It's always a good idea to follow the recommended shutdown procedure — otherwise work may be lost if files are not closed before shutting down. Hold down the Power/Lock key shown on page 12, then tap **Power off** as shown below.

Interacting with the Nexus 9

The main methods are:

- Tapping icons on the touch screen or tapping characters on the on-screen keyboard, using a finger or a *stylus*.
- *Voice recognition* using spoken search criteria or spoken text input e.g. for e-mail or word processing.
- An external Nexus 9 keyboard is available which also acts as a protective cover. Accessories such as alternative keyboards, etc., are discussed in the Appendix.

Touch Screen Gestures

- A single *tap* on an icon opens an app on the screen.
- Tap where you want to enter text and the *on-screen keyboard* pops up ready for you to start typing.
- *Swipe* or *slide* a finger across the screen quickly without hesitating, e.g., to scroll across the Home screen. Swiping can also unlock a locked screen and open the Quick Settings window. (Swipe down <u>twice</u> from the top.).
- *Touch and hold* an item such as an app or a widget, before sliding to a new position with the finger.
- *Double tap* to zoom in or zoom out of a screen. In some apps *pinching* two fingers together or *stretching* apart can be used to zoom out or zoom in. This is useful, for example, to enlarge a web page in Google Chrome or make an area easier to see in the Google Maps app.

The Menu Icon

The 3-dot menu icon shown on the right appears on many screens (in various colours). Tap this icon to see a list of options relevant to your current activity.

The On-Screen Keyboard

The touch screen method of controlling the computer works very well in most situations. The on-screen keyboard, shown below, pops up whenever you tap in a slot intended for the entry of text.

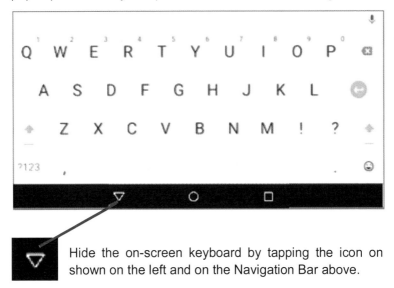

Hide the on-screen keyboard by tapping the icon on shown on the left and on the Navigation Bar above.

The Stylus

If you find accurate typing difficult using the on-screen keyboard, a cheap *stylus*, (around £2 or less) as shown below, may help. The stylus has a soft rubber tip to prevent damaging the screen.

Entering Text Using Voice Recognition

When entering text in an app such as Google Docs, as discussed in Chapter 9, the on-screen keyboard displays a microphone icon, as shown on the right and below. (You may need to tap the blank text area to display the icon when using Gmail, for example).

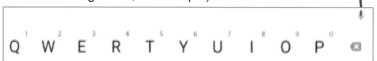

Tap the microphone icon to open the voice recognition window, ready for you to start speaking the text into the word processor or e-mail app, etc.

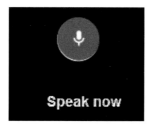

The Google Voice Search

As discussed later, when searching with Google, instead of typing the keywords for the search, tap the microphone icon as shown on the right and below.

This opens a window displaying the words **Speak now** and the icon shown on the right. Then speak the search keywords, such as "Charles Dickens", for example. The Nexus 9 responds with a list of links to web pages giving information about the great writer.

Using a Separate Keyboard

If you want to use the Nexus 9 like a laptop, you can buy a separate keyboard, as shown on the right. These include the Google Nexus 9 Keyboard Folio and various alternatives.

The keyboard doubles up as a case for the Nexus 9 and is held in place magnetically. *Bluetooth* is used to make the connection to the Nexus 9. As discussed in the Appendix, Bluetooth is a technology for connecting devices wirelessly over short distances.

The OTG (On The Go) Cable

This is an extremely useful accessory. The small connector on the right is inserted into the *Micro USB port* on the Nexus 9, shown on page 12. The large socket shown on the OTG cable is a standard *USB port* which can

be used to connect the following devices to the Nexus 9.

- Digital camera for viewing and transferring photos.
- SD card reader for extra storage and transferring files.
- USB *flash drive* or *memory stick* for transferring files.
- USB keyboard and mouse, connected using USB cables.
- USB dongle for a wireless keyboard and mouse.

The Appendix gives more details of accessories which can be connected to the Nexus 9. These include alternative keyboards and *pairing* to connect two Bluetooth devices.

Exploring the Nexus 9

The Home Screen

When you start the Nexus 9 by holding down the Power/Lock key and unlocking the screen, as discussed on pages 12 and 18, the *Home screen* opens as shown on the right. The Nexus 9 uses the latest Android 5 Lollipop operating system with new wallpaper patterns and screen colours known as *Material Design*.

There are several panels on the Home screen, viewable by sliding or swiping horizontally in either direction.

To launch an *app* or program, tap its icon on the Home screen.

A lot of apps are already installed on a new Nexus 9 and you can add more from the Play Store. Icons for your favourite apps can be placed on a personal Home screen for convenience.

The Navigation Bar at the bottom of every screen, is shown below. The left-hand icon opens the previous screen while the middle one opens the Home screen. The right-hand icon opens a revolving display of windows, each window showing a recently used app. Tap on a window to re-open the app.

The Favorites Tray

Along the bottom of the Home screen is the *Favorites* tray shown below, giving quick access to frequently used apps.

The icons on the Favorites tray above are as follows:

Google Mail is an extremely popular e-mail service, discussed in more detail later in this book.

The **Google Chrome** web browser is used to display and navigate web pages.

This icon displays the **All Apps** screen shown on the next page.

Tap this to watch popular **YouTube** online videos.

The **Photos** app stores and manages all your albums, photos and videos, as discussed in Chapter 8.

This launches either one of the two cameras on the Nexus 9, as discussed in detail in Chapter 8.

The **All Apps** icon above is a fixture on the Favorites tray — the others can all be replaced with apps of your own choice.

The All Apps Screen

When you tap the All Apps icon on the Favorites tray, shown on the right, an All Apps screen like the one below appears, displaying up to 30 apps. In fact you can have up to 3 similar All Apps screens as you add more apps from the Play Store, as discussed later in this chapter. Frequently used apps can be copied from the All Apps screens to make up a personal Home screen of your favourite apps.

More Apps

From the first All Apps screen, slide or swipe to the left to display a second All Apps screen. When you install new apps from the Play Store, their icons appear on this or a third All Apps screen. As mentioned previously, you can move apps around, delete some of them and insert new ones, as discussed in more detail shortly.

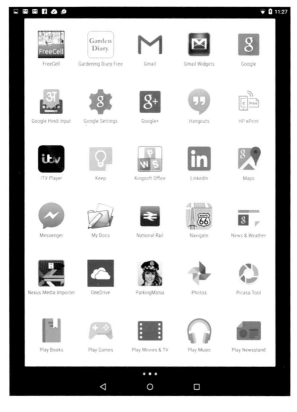

As shown above and on the All Apps screen on the previous page, there may be a lot of apps which you rarely use. For quick access, you can tailor the Favorites tray to include your most frequently used apps, as described on the next page.

Customising the Favorites Tray

The default Favorites tray on the Nexus 9 is shown below. The All Apps icon shown on the right and below is fixed on the Favorites tray. The other icons can be moved or deleted and replaced on the Favorites tray with apps of your own choice.

Removing an App from the Favorites Tray

Touch and hold the icon for the app you want to remove from the Favorites tray. Hold your finger on the icon until **X Remove** appears at the top of the screen. Without lifting your finger, drag the icon over **X Remove** and drop it, deleting the app or folder. Please note that removing an app from the Favorites tray doesn't uninstall the app from the Nexus 9. Its icon still appears on the All Apps screen. Alternatively, move an app from the Favorites tray and slide it onto another part of the Home screen.

Moving an App to the Favorites Tray

Clear a space on the Favorites tray by moving or removing an icon, as described above. To move an app on the Home screen to the Favorites tray, hold your finger over the icon, then drag the icon to the space on the Favorites tray. In the example below, the **Maps** icon has been added on the left. (You can have up to six apps of your own on the Favorites tray).

The red **YouTube** icon shown on the right and above has been removed and replaced by a circular *folder* icon shown on the lower right. This folder includes the **Facebook** app. Folders are discussed on the next page.

Apps within Folders

The circular icon shown on the right represents a *folder*, containing several apps. Folders can be created on the Home screen and also placed on the Favorites tray. For example, you might want to create a folder for all your games or all your music apps. Or you could put the  apps for **Facebook**, **Twitter** and **Skype**, shown below on the Home screen, in a folder called **Social**, for example.

On the Home screen, touch and drag the icons, one on top of the other, to form a single circular folder icon shown on the left below. Tap the folder icon to reveal the contents and to give a name to the folder. As shown below, tap **Unnamed Folder** and enter a name of your choice, such as **Social** in this example.

Tap a circular folder icon to view the apps within, as shown in the middle below. Then tap an icon to launch one of the apps.

Customising Your Home Screen

You can tailor your Home screen in the following ways:

- Change the background colour or wallpaper.
- Delete any apps and widgets you don't want.
- Copy from the All Apps screen any apps that you use regularly and place them on a personal Home screen.

Your personal Home screen can show just your most frequently used apps, in addition to those on the Favorites tray. To organise your apps further, you can group them in folders, as discussed on the previous page.

(The apps placed on the Home screen are only *copies*, so removing them from the Home screen doesn't remove them from the All Apps screen or uninstall them completely.)

Changing the Wallpaper on Your Home Screen

Hold your finger on an empty part of the Home screen until the following icons appear.

Tap the **WALLPAPERS** icon shown above then select a design from the samples at the bottom of the screen, as shown below. Tap **Pick image** on the left below to use a photo of your own.

Tap **Set wallpaper** at the top left of the screen to apply the new wallpaper, i.e. background, to the Home screen.

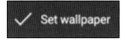

Deleting Apps from the Home Screen

You can safely remove redundant apps from the Home screen. Tap and hold the unwanted app until **X Remove** appears at the top of the screen. Then drag the app over **X Remove**. As the apps on the Home screen are only *copies*, they are still available on the All Apps screen.

Unlike the Home screen, care should be taken with the All Apps screen, where it is possible to *uninstall* apps completely. If the uninstalled apps are needed in the future, they will need to be reinstalled from the *Play Store*, as discussed shortly.

Adding Apps to Your Home Screen

To make up a personal Home screen with the apps you find most useful, open the Home screen where you want the apps to appear. Clear the screen of any apps and widgets you don't want. This is done by touching and holding the app or widget, then dragging onto **X Remove**, as described previously.

Tap the All Apps icon as shown on the right then touch and hold the app you want to move to the Home screen. The Home screen opens. Keeping your finger on the app, slide it into the required position on the Home screen. Part of a personal Home screen is shown below.

Widgets

A *widget* is an icon which is used to display information such as a calendar, your most recent e-mails, the weather or a clock, as shown on the right. Widgets appear alongside of apps on the Home screen, as shown on page 23. Tapping a widget displays more information, such as the weather forecast, on the full screen.

Viewing the Installed Widgets

Tap and hold an empty part of the Home screen until the **WIDGETS** icon appears, as shown in the centre below.

Tap the **WIDGETS** icon shown in the middle above to see the widgets already installed on the Nexus 9, such as the **Bookmarks** and **Calendar** widgets shown below.

Tap and hold a widget to add it to your Home screen. You can install more widgets from the Play Store, (after tapping **APPS/CATEGORIES/Widgets**) in the same way as apps, as described on the next page.

Getting Apps from the Play Store

Apps and widgets pre-installed on a new Nexus 9 can be supplemented by apps downloaded from the Play Store, either free or costing a few pounds. To open the Play Store, tap its icon shown on the right, on the All Apps screen or on the Home screen.

The Play Store

The Play Store has over a million of apps and widgets arranged in groups such as games, movies (to rent or buy), music, books and magazines (**NEWSSTAND**), as shown below.

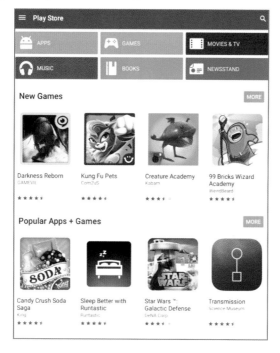

Scroll through the various **Categories** to find a particular app. Alternatively, you can carry out a search for an item such as an app, game, movie or book, etc., as discussed on the next page.

Searching the Play Store for Apps

As an example, a search will be made for an app to enable the Nexus 9 to be used as a music keyboard.

First tap **APPS**, as shown on the main Play Store screen shown on the previous page. Then tap the magnifying glass search icon, as shown on the right.

Typing the Keywords

The search bar appears as shown below, with a flashing cursor ready for you to type the name of the app or widget you wish to search for. The on-screen keyboard pops up automatically. Enter the keywords for the search, such as **music keyboard** and tap the search key (magnifying glass icon) on the keyboard.

The Voice Search

Tap the microphone icon shown on the right. The small window shown below appears, requiring you to speak the keywords, such as **music keyboard**.

The speech recognition system on the Nexus 9 is most impressive and immediately finds lots of music keyboard apps, as shown on the next page. You might like to practise searching for a few apps using the microphone. Apps I found in this way included **chess game**, **route planner** and **sound recorder**.

Downloading and Installing Apps

The search for music keyboards results in a long list of apps, as shown in the sample below. Most of these are free.

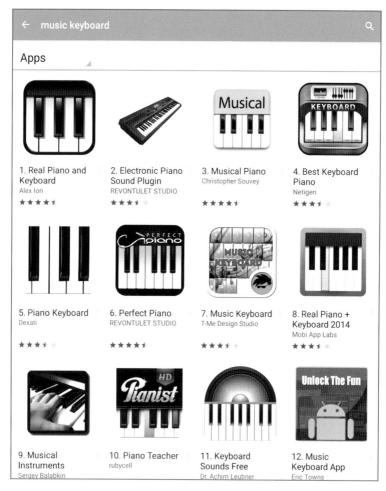

To obtain an app, first tap its icon as shown above. If it's free, the word **INSTALL** appears on the right. If there is a charge, the price is shown on the right, instead of **INSTALL**.

For a free app, tap **INSTALL** to download the app to your Nexus 9. An icon for the app is placed on your All Apps screen and on your Home screen. The app should now be ready to use.

If there is a charge for an app, tap the price and you will then need to buy it by providing your bank details, before proceeding to install it as before.

Deleting Apps from the All Apps Screen

After touching and holding an app you previously installed, the word **Uninstall** appears at the top of the screen, next to a dustbin icon, as shown below.

If you slide the app over the dustbin icon or **Uninstall**, the app will be removed from the Nexus 9. If you need the app again you will need to reinstall it from the Play Store.

Default Apps or widgets are those already installed on the All Apps screens when the Nexus 9 was purchased. These default apps and widgets do not have the **Uninstall** option when you touch and hold their icons in the All Apps screen. Only the words **App info** appear at the top of the screen, allowing you to view details about the app and also there is an option to **DISABLE** the app.

Key Points: Apps and Widgets

- The Nexus 9 is "driven" by tapping icons representing apps and widgets.

- Apps are small applications or programs such as a web browser, a game or a drawing program.

- Widgets are small windows, usually displaying information such as a calendar, news or an e-mail inbox.

- The All Apps screen shows all of the apps installed on the Nexus 9.

- The Home screen consists of several panels which can be customized to display selected apps and widgets.

- Apps and widgets can be copied to the Home screen by touching and holding, then sliding onto the Home screen.

- Further apps and widgets can be downloaded from the Google Play Store. New apps are placed on the All Apps screen and the Home screen automatically.

- At the bottom of every Home screen is a Favorites tray which displays 6 icons for frequently used apps.

- The user can change 6 of the apps on the Favorites tray.

- The Favorites tray also displays the All Apps icon.

- Widgets cannot be placed on the Favorites tray.

- Related apps can be grouped together and placed in folders, such as Painting, Photography, Games, etc.

- Folder icons are circular, can have a name and can be placed on the Favorites tray.

- Apps on the Home screen are only copies. Deleting them doesn't remove them from the All Apps screen.

- The Navigation Bar at the bottom of all the screens has icons to open the Home screen, to display the last screen visited and show recently used apps in rotating windows.

4

Further Features

Introduction

This chapter looks at some more of the features built into the Nexus 9 and, more precisely, its Android operating system. The features described in this chapter are:

Google Now and Google Cards

This feature provides Google searching for information using both voice and text queries. Google Cards automatically displays useful, real-time information for your current location.

Settings

Used to switch important settings on and off, make adjustments and tailor the Nexus 9 to your own requirements.

Notifications

This screen keeps you up-to-date with new e-mail messages, calendar events, new downloads. Also Bluetooth, Wi-Fi, battery strength and aeroplane mode, as discussed shortly.

My Library

This is a widget that displays all the books, movies, music, etc., that are already on your Nexus 9.

Calendar

Keeps track of all your appointments and sends reminders of imminent events, synchronised to your various devices.

Google Maps and Sat Nav

Displays maps of anywhere in the world, including Satellite View and Google Earth. Using the built-in Global Positioning System the Nexus 9 can be used as a *Sat Nav*.

Google Now

This is an extension to the popular Google search engine. Google Now employs GPS (Global Positioning System) satellite technology to pinpoint your exact, current location. This is used to gather local information such as the weather and traffic conditions.

Google Now doesn't require any setting up. You just need to make sure **Location** is switched on in the **Settings** and **Mode** is set to **High accuracy** as discussed on pages 43 and 44.

To open Google Now, swipe up from the bottom of the screen, or tap the Google icon on the All Apps screen, shown on the right. You can also open Google Now by swiping right from the Home screen. The Google Now screen opens with a search bar across the top, as shown below.

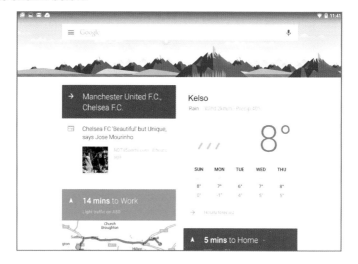

As shown above, Google Now displays a series of panels known as *Google cards*, relating to your current location or recent searches with Google.

Searching in Google Now

Typing Keywords

The search bar in Google Now shown below allows you to enter the keywords for a search, such as **weather in Florence** for example, by typing using the on-screen keyboard.

Spoken Queries

You can also tap the microphone icon, as shown above and on the right. Then speak your query into the Nexus 9. Using spoken queries is discussed in more detail on page 33. The results of the search may produce a spoken answer, as well as a Google Card, as shown above. You will also see some traditional Google results as shown below, which you can tap to open web pages relevant to your search.

Weather in Florence, Italy | 14 day weather outlook of Florence
www.worldweatheronline.com/Florence-weather/Toscana/IT.aspx
Latest **weather in Florence** Weather, Italy. Florence 14 day weather forecast, historical weather, weather map and Florence holiday weather forecast.
Weather Map - Florence, Italy weather - Monthly Averages

Perhaps you could experiment with a few spoken queries. For example, I said "tabby cat" with the microphone selected and received a spoken answer and a list of traditional Google search results with links to web pages, as shown below.

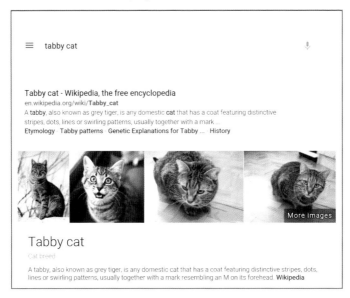

Sporting Fixtures

If you enter or speak the name of a favourite sports team, such as Chelsea FC or Manchester United, Google Now gives the latest result and details of their next fixture.

Google Search Icons

The two icons for searching shown below are used regularly on the Nexus 9. You can also launch a voice search from the Home screen by saying "Ok Google" .

Google Search

Google Voice Search

More on Google Cards

Google Cards pop up on the Google Now screen without you taking any action. For example, suppose you enquire about flights at your local airport, or about traffic on local roads. Google Now responds with Google Cards based on your recent activities. Google Cards are continually updated automatically, giving reminders of imminent events from you Calendar, fixtures for your favourite teams and news on topics you've been researching. You may also receive weather news based on your current location identified by the Nexus 9's built-in *GPS* (*Global Positioning System* based on information from satellites).

After you swipe up from the bottom of the screen, Google Now display cards based on your previous activities and interests, such as the football results and share prices shown below.

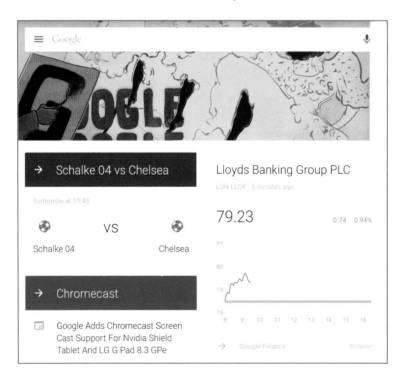

The Google Now Menu

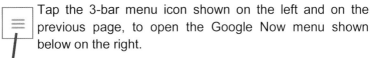

Tap the 3-bar menu icon shown on the left and on the previous page, to open the Google Now menu shown below on the right.

Reminders can be created to pop up on Google Now when a particular event is imminent.

Customise allows you to select topics for which you wish to receive updates in Google Now, under the headings **Sports**, **Stocks**, **Places**, **TV & video**, etc.

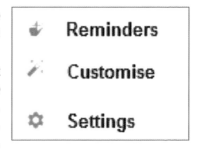

Settings above opens a sub-menu for Google Search and Google Cards. This allows you to switch Google Now Off and set various search and other options. (Switching Google Now On is discussed on the next page).

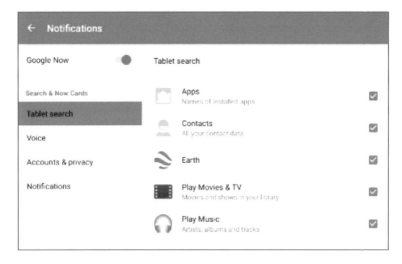

Making Sure Google Now is On

In order to use Google Now displaying cards as shown on page 41, a number of features need to be switched on. These are probably already switched on by default, but you can easily check, as shown below. The main settings needed to fully use Google Now are:

- Google Now: **ON**
- Location: **ON**
- Location Mode: **High accuracy**

If Google Now is Off, when you swipe up from the bottom, or tap the Google icon on the Home screen, you only see the basic Google screen, not the more colourful Google Now screen, as shown on page 41.

Switching Google Now On

Swipe up from the bottom of the screen. If Google Now is Off, the words GET GOOGLE NOW appear in a box across the screen. Tap this box and the **Get Google Now** screen appears, as shown below. Tap **YES, I'M IN**, as shown at the bottom right below to turn Google Now On.

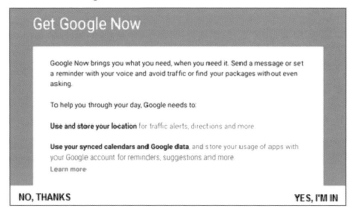

Switching Location (GPS, etc.) On

Swipe down twice from the top of the screen to display the **Quick Settings** panel shown on page 45. You should see the **Location** icon in white, if **Location** is switched On.

To make sure **Location** is On, tap the **SETTINGS** icon as discussed on page 16 and then under **Personal** tap **Location**, as shown below.

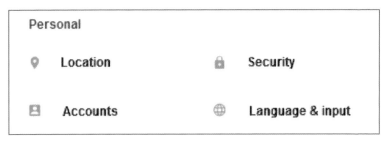

The following screen opens, allowing you to make sure **Location** services are **On**, if necessary by tapping the circular button on the right.

Tap **Mode** shown above and from the window which opens as shown below, tap the button to select **High accuracy**. This makes sure that **GPS**, **Wi-Fi** and **mobile networks** are all used to identify your current location.

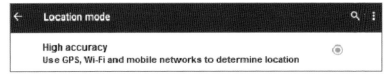

Quick Settings

Swipe down twice from the top of the screen to display the **Quick Settings** panel shown below. The icons in the lower half of the panel are bright white when a function is switched on and greyed out when the function is switched off, as shown below. Tap a greyed out icon when you want to switch the function on.

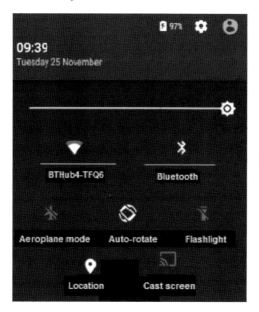

 This icon, at the top right of the Quick Settings panel above, gives the state of charge of the battery.

 Tap this icon, also shown at the top right above, to open the main Settings screen shown on page 47.

 New users can be added to a Nexus 9 after tapping the icon on the left and on the top right above.

Beneath the time and date shown above is a brightness control, as shown below. Use a finger to slide the icon.

BTHub4-TFQ6 (Router)

The icon shown on the left and on the Quick Settings panel on the previous page is used to display your router and to switch Wi-Fi On and Off, as discussed in Chapter 2.

Bluetooth

After tapping this icon you can switch **Bluetooth** On and Off. Connecting Bluetooth devices to the Nexus 9 is discussed in the appendix.

Aeroplane mode

Aeroplane mode switches the Internet Off for flight safety. Any books, etc., to be read on a flight need to be downloaded to the Nexus 9 before boarding the plane.

Auto-rotate

Tapping the **Auto-rotate** button alternates between allowing the screen to rotate when the Nexus 9 is turned into landscape mode or keeping it fixed relative to the sides in portrait mode, as discussed on page 17.

Flashlight

The flash LED (shown on page 12) for the rear camera on the Nexus 9 is switched On and Off using this icon.

Location

Location allows Google to determine your current location, as discussed on page 44.

Chromecast

This icon can be used to mirror your Nexus 9 screen onto an HDMI TV screen, using the Google **Chromecast** dongle, as discussed in the Appendix.

Please Note: For clarity most of the icons are shown in clear white above, indicating they are On or selected. In practice, several of the icons on the Quick Settings panel will be greyed out for much of the time, such as **Aeroplane mode** and **Flashlight**, as shown on page 45.

The Main Settings Screen

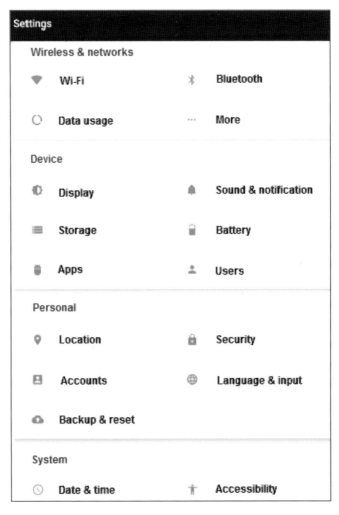

As discussed on page 16 and 45, the **Settings** screen shown above can be launched by tapping its icon on the Quick Settings panel or the similar icon on the All Apps screen, as shown on the right.

Notifications

Swipe down from the top of any screen to see your **Notifications** as shown below. These keep you up-to-date with, for example, your latest e-mails, calendar events, files received, devices connected and updates available, as shown below. Tap on a notification title for more information or to take further action. Tap outside of the notifications to close the panel.

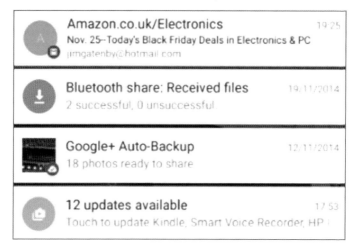

Small notifications appear on the top left of the screen, as shown here on the right. In this sample, reading from the  left, there are notifications of a screenshot captured, a video download completed, a PDF file downloaded and finally a Google+ notification.

The System Tray

This is a group of icons on the top right of the screen, as shown here on the right. In this example, reading from the left,  there are icons showing Bluetooth On, Wi-Fi On and connection strength, followed by the battery state of charge and the time.

My Library

This is a widget that allows you to display all the music, magazines, books, and movies that are installed on a Nexus 9. Some of these media may be already installed from new or you may have added more from the Google Play Store.

The **My Library** widget may already be displayed on one of your Home screens. If not, open the **Widgets** screen as described on page 31 and scroll across until you see the **Play – My Library** widget as shown on the right. Touch and hold this widget, then slide into a convenient place on the Home screen. The **Play-My Library** window opens as shown below on the right, to display icons giving access to all of your installed media, i.e., **My music**, **My books**, etc. Tap **My Library** shown on the right to place the **My Library** widget on the Home screen, as shown below.

Tap any of the icons, **My music**, **My books**, **My newsstand**, or **My movies & TV**, to open your chosen medium.

To make room for **My Library**, widgets and apps which you no longer need can be deleted from the Home screen by holding and sliding over **X Remove** at the top of the screen.

The Calendar

The Calendar on the Nexus 9 includes the following features:

- Keeping a record of all your future events.
- Sending you notifications of imminent events.
- Synchronizing changes between various devices, such as your Nexus 9, smartphone, laptop or desktop PC or Mac.

The Calendar is opened by tapping its icon, shown on the right, on the All Apps screen. The Calendar opens as shown at the bottom right below. A 3-dot menu button, shown on the right, at the top right of the calendar, opens the menu shown on the left below. This has options to display **Days**, **Weeks or Months**. **Schedule** lists your events in a list which can be scrolled vertically.

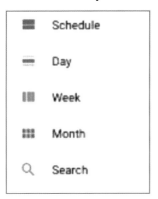

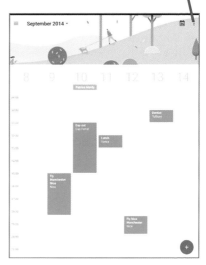

Scroll through the days, weeks or months by swiping horizontally.

Creating a New Event or Editing an Event

Tap the **New event** icon, shown on the right and at the bottom right of the calendar on the previous page. Now enter the details of the event such as the title, time and place.

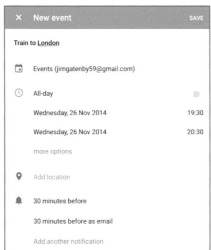

At the bottom of the **New event** screen you can set a reminder in the form of a notification or an e-mail. With a notification there is a beep and then an event, such as **Train to London** in this example, appears in the **Notifications** panel, as discussed on page 48. Tap the event name for further details.

To edit an existing event, double-tap the event's title on the Calendar, then tap the pencil icon which appears, as shown on the right. This opens the **Edit event** screen allowing you to amend the details.

The Calendar Widget

A Calendar widget appears in the WIDGETS screen, as discussed on page 31. This can be copied to a suitable clear space on the Home screen. This is done by touching and holding the widget and then sliding into position on the Home screen, as described in more detail on page 31. The Calendar widget lists all your forthcoming events, automatically updated with information from the Calendar app.

Calendar widget

Tap the Calendar widget to open the Calendar app full screen for editing existing entries or adding new events.

Syncing Your Nexus 9 Calendar with a PC, etc.

The Google Calendar can be viewed on all the common platforms — Nexus 9, Nexus 7, iPad, laptop or desktop PC or Mac, etc. On a PC or Mac open **www.google.co.uk**. If necessary **Sign in** with your Gmail address (or **Sign up** for a new one). Then select the **Apps** icon on the top right of the screen, shown here on the right. From the drop-down window which appears, select the **Calendar** icon, shown below, to open the Calendar.

New events can be added to the Calendar on any of your devices. Any changes to the Calendar are automatically synced across to all the devices you are signed in to with your Gmail address and password.

Google Maps

The Nexus 9 has an icon for Google Maps already installed on the All Apps screen, as shown on the right. When you first tap the **Maps** icon, it opens to show a map of your current area. To find a map of another area, enter a *place name* or *post code* in

the search bar. In this example, **Farne Islands** was entered. Stretch or pinch the map with two fingers to zoom in or zoom out.

Tap the 3-bar menu icon, shown above, on the top left of the screen, to see a menu of alternative views of the area, i.e. **Satellite**, **Terrain** and **Google Earth**, as shown on the right below.

Terrain is the basic map view shown above on the right. Both **Satellite** and **Google Earth** display satellite images of the area. **Google Earth** has another menu, shown below on the left, allowing you to display additional information, such as businesses, places of interest, etc., as shown on the right below.

Using the Nexus 9 and Google Maps as a Sat Nav

The built-in *GPS* in the Nexus 9 is used for identifying your precise location when planning a journey and also en route. Make sure **Location/GPS** is switched On, as shown on page 44. If your Nexus 9 is Wi-Fi only, set up a route *before* setting off, i.e. while still connected to the Internet. In Google maps, tap the 3-bar menu icon and select your mode of transport.

Enter the name or post code of your destination. Google Maps responds with the travelling time from your current location. Tap the time (e.g. **4hr 15 min** shown on the right). Traffic disruptions are listed, together with alternative routes which can be viewed by tapping the map shown below.

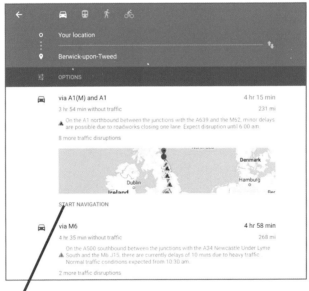

Tap **START NAVIGATION** shown above to start receiving spoken directions for each stage of your journey.

There are several other Sat Nav apps available in the Google Play Store discussed in Chapter 3, such as Navfree and CoPilot.

Entertainment

Introduction

Amongst many other things, the Nexus 9 is a versatile entertainment platform. The following activities are discussed in this chapter:

- eBooks — electronic books which may be downloaded from the Internet for reading offline at any time.

- Music, magazines, movies and games downloaded for free or bought or rented.

- YouTube — a Google website which streams videos uploaded by the public and by commercial companies.

- Live and catchup TV and radio.

The small size and light weight of the Nexus 9 mean you can use it literally anywhere — on a sofa, in bed or in a public place such as a restaurant. You can stow it in a bag and take it on holiday; many places such as hotels and restaurants now have free Wi-Fi so while you're away you can still go online for all your favourite Internet activities. The Nexus 9 may also be used for your personal in-flight entertainment, if your airline allows it. *Aeroplane mode* or *flight mode* must be switched on to prevent possible interference with the aircraft's instruments. This was discussed on page 46 and only allows you to use the Nexus 9 *offline*, i.e. not connected to the Internet. Such offline activities would include reading an eBook or watching movies which have been saved for offline use, before boarding the aircraft.

eBooks

Many 20th century projects involved devices for reading books electronically on a screen. The Amazon Kindle, introduced in 2007, quickly became a best-seller, being extremely light and affordable and an efficient alternative to the printed book. Millions of eBooks are available to be downloaded from the Amazon Kindle Store and saved on a tablet such as the Nexus 9. The Nexus 9 can store far more books than most people are ever likely to read. (Figures in the thousands have been quoted, depending on what you take as the average size of an eBook).

- The Nexus 9 has its own app, *Play Books*, for reading eBooks and you can use it to download books from the Google Play Store, which contains millions of titles.

- You can also install the free Kindle App on the Nexus 9 and obtain books from the Amazon Kindle Store.

You can always delete any eBooks you no longer want, to save space on the internal storage of the Nexus 9.

Google Play Books

When you first start to use the Nexus 9, there is already an icon for the Play Books app on the All Apps screen, shown on the right. If you read a lot of eBooks you may wish to copy the icon to the Favorites tray on the Home screen, as shown below. Changing the apps on the Favorites tray is discussed on page 27.

Play Books

Tap the Play Books app shown at the bottom of the previous page, then tap at the top left of the screen to display the menu shown on the right

Tap **My Library** to see all the books you've bought and to see samples recommended by Google.

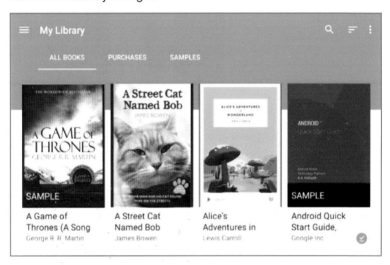

Tap **Shop** to open the Play Store as shown on the next page.

The Book section of the Play Store can also be opened by tapping the icon shown on the right, on the All Apps screen, then selecting **Books**, as shown below.

To search for a particular book, tap the magnifying glass icon shown on the right and at the top right of **My Library** shown above.

This opens the Play Store shown on the next page, displaying books which match your search criteria.

Books in the Play Store

In the Play Store you can browse through the various categories listed down the left, as shown below, check new arrivals and best selling books or look at the top free books.

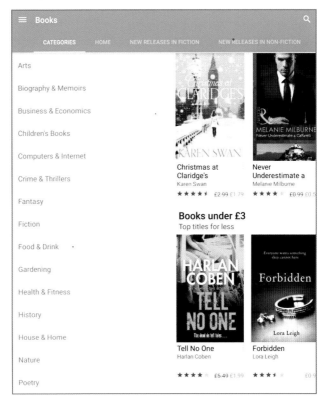

Alternatively you can search for a particular book after tapping the search icon shown on the right and above. Type the title of the book, replacing **Search**
Google Play shown below. Or tap the microphone icon shown in the middle below and <u>speak</u> the title of the book.

For example, a search for **Bradshaws Guide** produced numerous results, as shown in the small sample below. Tap a book cover for more details or to buy the book. Alternatively tap the 3-dot menu button shown below, to the right of the book title, to add the book to a *wishlist* or to buy it. Some of the publications on this particular subject are free.

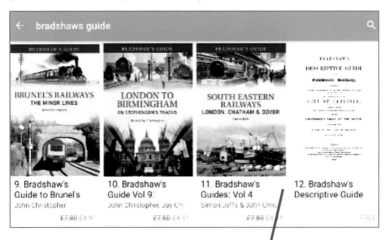

The 3-dot menu button on the lower right of a book cover is shown enlarged on the right. If the book's free, the option to add it to your library in the clouds appears, as well as the option to add it to your wishlist.

Add to library

Add to wishlist

If a book is not free, the option to buy the book is displayed. As shown on the right some books have an option to read some free *sample* pages.

Buy £4.91

Free sample

Add to wishlist

Once you've obtained a book, a small white tick on a blue shopping bag icon appears to the right of the title on the book's cover in the Play Store.

Once you've obtained a book, it's available for you to read from your Library in the clouds. Books in the clouds must be read when you're online. To read a book where there is no Wi-Fi, you need to download a copy of the book and save it in the internal storage of the Nexus 9. In My Library below, the right-hand book cover has a white tick in a blue circle, indicating that the book has been downloaded to the Internal Storage of the Nexus 9.

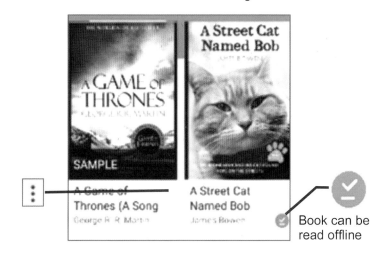

Book can be read offline

Downloading a Book for Reading Offline

The book on the left above has no tick, as shown on the right-hand book. To make the book available offline, tap the cover of the book or tap the 3-dot menu button shown above and then tap **Download**.

Download

Delete from library

About this book

Deleting a Book

A book saved on the internal storage of the Nexus 9 can be removed after tapping the 3-dot menu button shown above and selecting **Remove download**. Tap **Delete from library** to remove the book from the clouds.

Remove download

Delete from library

About this book

Reading an eBook

Tap the Play Books app on the Favorites tray, or on the All Apps screen, to open My Library or Read Now, as discussed on page 57. Then tap the cover of the book you want to read. The book opens on the screen. Scroll backwards and forwards through the pages by swiping to the left

Play Books

or right, or tapping in the left and right margins. Tap anywhere on the text of the current page to view information about the page and to display various icons, etc., as shown in the top and bottom margins below. Tap anywhere over the text again to switch off the icons and information.

Drag the blue ball on the slider shown below to advance rapidly forward or backward through the book.

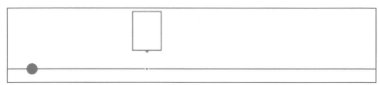

Tap the page thumbnail shown above to return to the page you were previously reading.

Across the top of the page, as shown above and on the previous page, the book title, author, chapter title and page number are displayed. The icons on the top right above have the following functions:

 Search for certain words and highlight them where they occur in the text.

 List chapter headings, page numbers and bookmarks.

 Change the brightness and formatting such as size of text, line spacing and font, etc.

 Open the menu shown on page 63, including options to add or remove a bookmark.

Bookmarks

Tap in the right-hand corner of the screen to add a bookmark in the top right-hand corner, as shown on the right. Tap a bookmark to remove it.

Using the Nexus 9 as a Talking Book

The Play Books app on the Nexus 9 has a **Read Aloud** option. This feature can be used with many of the books and magazines in the Play Store. (As discussed on page 65, magazines can be obtained from the NEWSSTAND section of the Play Store).

To start reading aloud:

- Tap the cover of the book in My Library or Read Now.
- Tap anywhere on the text of a page to display the icons shown on page 62.
- Tap the 3-dot menu button also shown on page 62.
- From the menu which appears, tap **Read aloud**, as shown below on the right

The Nexus 9 will now start reading the book aloud. To finish, tap over the text to display the 3-dot menu button and tap to display the menu shown on the right, but which now displays **Stop reading aloud**.

Original pages

About this book

Share

Add bookmark

Read aloud

Settings

Help & feedback

If you tap a book or magazine in My Library or Read Now, which is not compatible with this feature, the menu displays, in greyed out text, **Read aloud unavailable**.

Tapping **Settings** shown on the right opens a menu which includes options to use the volume key (shown on page 12) to turn pages and to use a "more natural voice."

Original pages shown in the above menu displays a *scanned image* of the original book in the *PDF* (Portable Document Format) file format. Normally eBooks are saved in the *ePub* file format, also known as *flowing text*. The **Original pages** option does not appear on the above menu on some books.

The Kindle App for the Nexus 9

To read eBooks in the popular Kindle format is just a case of installing the Kindle app from the Google Play Store. Tap the Play Store shopping bag icon, shown on
the right, on the All Apps screen. Then tap **APPS** and tap the magnifying glass search icon. Type **Kindle** into the search bar or tap the microphone icon and say **Kindle** to display a list of Kindle apps, as shown in the sample above.

Tap the Amazon Kindle app shown on the left above and tap **INSTALL** to put an icon, shown on the right, on your All Apps and Home screen. Sign in with an
e-mail address and password for an Amazon account or create a new account.

Tap **Store** at the top right of the screen to open the Amazon Book Store of over 2 million books. If you already have an account with Amazon, you can buy books very easily using **Buy Now with 1-Click**.

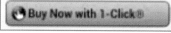

To start reading one of the Kindle books you already have, tap the front cover.

Reading Magazines

Open the Play Store after tapping its icon, as shown on the right, on the Home screen or the All Apps screen.

The Play Store has a **NEWSSTAND** feature, as shown below on the right and on page 32, where you can buy or subscribe to magazines in various categories. Some free magazines are also available.

Magazines are installed in a similar way to books, as just described. To start reading a magazine in your library, tap **MY LIBRARY** on the Home screen, then tap **My Newsstand** shown on the right, as discussed on page 49.

Music on the Nexus 9

The methods used for obtaining and listening to music are very similar to those just described for books and magazines. Open the Play Store as described and tap **MUSIC** as shown above.

Then browse for the music you want, using the various **GENRES**, such as **Classical**, **Folk** or **Pop** and **TOP ALBUMS**, **NEW RELEASES** or **TOP SONGS**, etc.

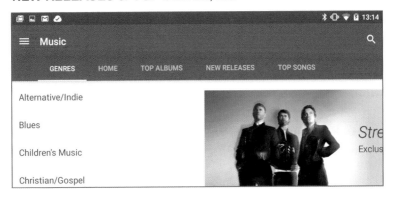

Alternatively tap the magnifying glass search icon, shown below, then enter the name of the record or artist. You can type the words or tap the microphone icon and speak them.

You can buy singles as shown on the right, or albums. Tap the cover to buy the single or album. Also shown is the familiar 3-dot menu icon which, in this example, displays options to **Add to wishlist** or **Buy £0.99**.

Fall Down At Your Feet
Take That
£0.99

After tapping to buy a piece of music it is added to your library in the clouds, as discussed earlier. Then it can be

played after opening the music app by tapping the headset icon shown on the left, located on the All Apps or Home screen.

The control bar along the bottom of the Nexus 9 music screen has the usual Play, Forward, Back and Pause buttons.

The volume control key on the side of the Nexus 9 is shown on page 12. Tap the 3-dot menu icon on the right on the artwork of the music to display a list of options, including **Download** shown on the right below. This will save the music on your Nexus 9, not just in the clouds, allowing you to play the music when you're offline, i.e. not connected to the Internet.

Start instant mix

Shuffle

Play next

Add to queue

Add to playlist

Download

Google Play Movies & TV

The Play Store contains a range of movies and TV shows in various categories, etc., as shown below.

A movie may be bought or rented and you may have to begin watching a movie within 30 days of renting it and the rental may expire 48 hours after you start watching it.

To add a movie to a **Wishlist** for consideration later, tap the icon shown on the right and on the screenshot above. Alternatively tap **RENT** or **BUY** and after completing the transaction, the movie will be available in your Library. To watch the movie, tap the **Play Movies & TV** icon shown on the right, on the All Apps screen, then tap the movie graphic and tap the **Play** button.

Downloading a Movie for Viewing Offline

To make a movie watchable offline, tap the **Download** icon on the movie graphic, shown on the right. The circle starts to fill with red "ink" and when completely full the download is complete. The icon then displays a white tick in a red circle, as shown on the left and below. A *notification* of the download should also be displayed when you swipe down from the top of the screen, as discussed on page 48.

YouTube

YouTube is a website, owned by Google, which provides a platform for individuals, as well as commercial organisations, to share videos which they've made. These can rapidly "go viral" when millions of people watch them around the world.

To launch YouTube, tap the icon shown on the right. If the icon is not present on your Nexus 9, it can be downloaded from the Play Store and installed as described on pages 33-36. The YouTube screen shows a long list of video clips which can be scrolled up and down by swiping. Swipe from left to right to display the menu shown below.

To watch a video, tap a menu option such as **Popular on YouTube** or **Sport** and, if necessary, scroll vertically to display the cover picture and title of the required video. Tap the picture to start the video. To pause a video, tap the screen and then tap the pause button.

Live and Catchup Television and Radio

The Google Play Store includes the free BBC iPlayer app, as shown on the right. This can be installed from the Play Store using the methods described on pages 33-36. Tap the icon shown on the right to open the BBC iPlayer as shown below.

BBC iPlayer

The row of icons on the upper right above enable you to search for and download programmes, switch between TV and radio and mark programmes as favourite. Tap the 3-dot menu button shown on the right and above to display the menu above on the right, which gives options to watch or listen to live TV and radio. Otherwise go back and watch or listen to programs broadcast previously, as shown below.

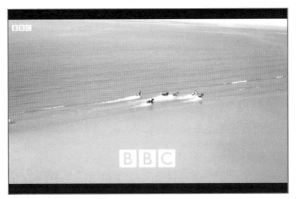

Nexus 9 Games

The Google Play Store contains lots of free or inexpensive games in various categories, as shown below.

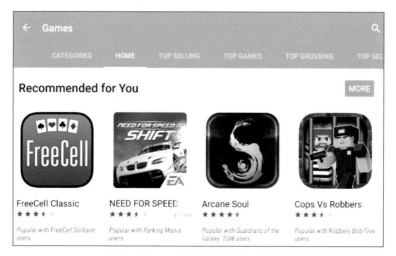

Games are installed as apps on your All Apps and Home screens, as discussed on pages 33-36. To launch a game, tap its icon, as shown on the right.

You may wish to group all of your games into one or more folders, as discussed on page 28. Tap the resulting circular folder icon to open the folder and give it a name. For quick access, the folder icon can be placed on the Favorites tray by sliding it into a gap created by sliding away another app, as discussed on page 27. In the example below, the games folder has been placed on the extreme left of the Favorites tray.

Browsing the Web

Introduction

The Nexus 9 gives you access to millions of web pages containing the latest high quality information on any subject you care to think of.

The *Google Chrome web browser* enables you to search the millions of web pages quickly and easily and displays the results in an attractive and readable format. Closely associated with Chrome, *Google Search* is the world's leading web search app on all platforms – tablet, laptop and desktop computers. The Nexus 9, which uses the standard Google Android operating system, is an ideal tool for browsing the Internet using Google Chrome. In my opinion this rewarding and useful activity alone justifies the purchase of the Nexus 9, not to mention its many other functions such as news, social networking and entertainment, discussed elsewhere in this book.

Some of the main functions of Google Chrome are:

- To search for and display information after entering or speaking *keywords* into the Google search engine.

- To access web pages after entering their *address* such as **www.babanibooks.com** into the browser.

- To move between web pages by tapping *links*, also known as *hyperlinks*, on a web page and move forward and backwards between web pages.

- To *bookmark* web pages for revisiting at a later time.

Launching Google Chrome

To launch Google Chrome, tap its icon on the Home or All Apps screen or on the Favorites tray, shown below.

The **Welcome to Google Chrome** screen opens, as shown below. Tap **Take a tour** to view several pages of notes to help you get started.

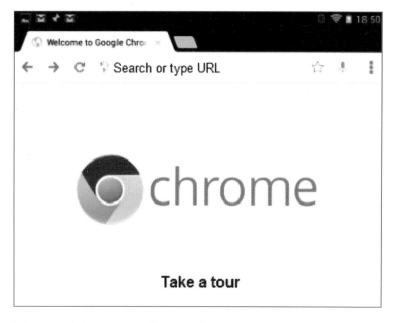

The search bar across the top of the screen is the place to start your web browsing activities. Here you enter either the address of a website or *keywords* which should pinpoint the subject you are interested in.

Entering the Address of a Web Site

Every website has a unique address, known as its *URL*, or *Uniform Resource Locator*. A typical web address is:

www.babanibooks.com

Type the URL into the search bar, as shown below and tap the Go key, shown on the right.

For a complicated address you may need to enter the URL in full. However, in practice you don't often need to be too pedantic; simply entering **babanibooks**, for example, will lead you to the required website. If you've visited a site before, it may appear in a list of suggested sites which pops up to save you typing time.

After entering the address of the website and tapping the Go key on the on-screen keyboard shown at the top right, the site's Home Page opens on the screen, as shown in the extract below.

The Voice Search

Instead of typing the URL, as discussed above, tap the microphone icon shown on the right, then speak the web address.

The Keyword Search

This is used to find out about a particular subject rather than visiting a website whose address you know, as discussed on the previous page. The World Wide Web seems to contain pages on every conceivable subject. For example, suppose you wanted to find out about the Border Reivers, who were a major part of the turbulent past in the borders between England and Scotland. Simply enter **border reivers** into the Google Chrome search bar, as shown below. (There's no need to use capital letters when entering search criteria — **Border Reivers** and **border reivers** produce the same results).

After tapping the Go key on the on-screen keyboard, the screen displays a list of Google search results, as shown in the small sample below.

A search often yields millions of results although many may be irrelevant. For example, historians studying the Border Reivers may not be interested in the website of the Border Reivers Rambling Club which might appear in the results. Google puts the most relevant results near the top of the list.

Each of the blue headings on a search result represents a *link* to a web page containing the keywords, **Border Reivers** in this example. Tap a link to have a look at the website.

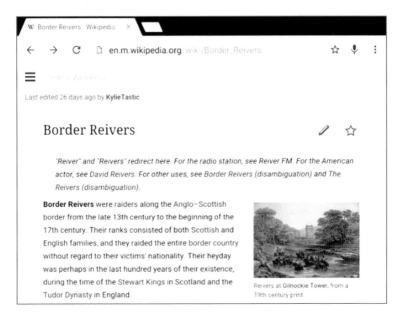

Surfing the Net

On the web page shown above, some words are highlighted in blue. These are *links* which can be tapped to open further web pages. Each new page will probably have lots of further links, so tapping these will open a succession of web pages.

Try typing a few diverse keywords into Google Chrome and see how easy it is to find good information on virtually any subject, no matter how bizarre. Here's a few to get you started:

capability brown	red squirrel	entrevaux
making elderberry wine	samuel johnson	airbus a380
st paul de vence	hadron collider	shearing a sheep

The Internet is surely the world's largest and most up-to-date encyclopaedia covering almost every known subject. At a more practical level, Google Chrome is probably the DIY enthusiast's best friend. Type any DIY task, such as **mending a puncture**, for example, and numerous websites offer helpful advice, often including step-by-step videos.

Previously Visited Pages

The back and forward buttons shown on the right and below allow you to quickly move between recently visited pages. Tapping the circular arrow **Refresh** button on the right and below loads the latest version of a web page. (For speed, the Chrome browser may initially load an earlier web page which is then replaced).

As you move forward or back between web pages, the keywords from each search, such as **shearing a sheep**, are displayed on a tab at the top left of the screen, as shown above and below.

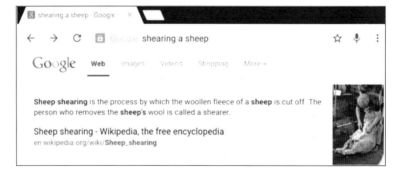

Tabbed Browsing

When you do a search in Google Chrome and then proceed to surf the web, as described earlier, there is only one tab displaying the current web page, as described at the bottom of the previous page. However, Chrome allows you to open each web page in a tab of its own, so that all the tabs are visible along the top of the screen, as shown in the example below.

This makes it easy to move straight to a particular web page, rather than moving through them all one at a time using the back and forward buttons. Tap a tab to open that web page. With a large number of web pages open, the tabs are stacked on top of each other and can be moved around by sliding or gently swiping left or right.

Opening a Web Page in Its Own New Tab

Tap the **New tab** icon shown on the right and below.

A **New tab** appears, as shown above on the right, with the search bar ready for you to enter your search criteria by typing or speaking. After carrying out the search and selecting a web page from the results, this page appears on its own tab. The search criteria, in this case **green woodpecker**, appear on the top of the tab, as shown below, replacing the words **New tab**.

Using the Google Search App

In the previous examples, Google Chrome was opened by tapping its icon on the Favorites tray. You can also launch Chrome after tapping the Google icon shown on the right, on the All Apps screen. Then enter the search criteria, such as **honey buzzard sightings** in this example, in the Google search bar, as shown below.

Google

☰   **honey buzzard sightings**   🎤

Tap on a link in the search results to open a web page you want to look at. The web page opens in Google Chrome, in a new tab of its own, **Honey Buzzard**, in this example, as shown below.

To switch to another web page from a previous search, simply tap its tab, such as **mending a puncture**, partly shown above.

Closing a Tab

Close a tab by tapping the cross, as shown below.

Bookmarking a Web Page

You can create a series of *bookmarks* so that you can quickly return to your favourite web pages at any time in the future. With the required web page open on the screen, tap the star shaped bookmark icon as shown on the right and on the right of the search bar below.

The **Add Bookmark** window opens, allowing you to name the bookmark or accept the name suggested by Chrome. Tap **Save** to add the web page to the **Mobile Bookmarks** page. To view the bookmarks, tap the 3-dot menu icon shown on the right and then tap **Bookmarks** on the drop-down menu.

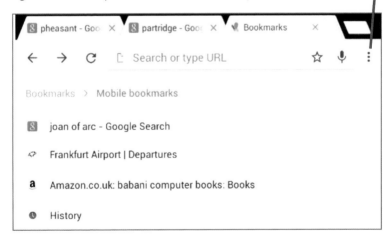

To open one of the bookmarked web pages, tap its icon on the **Bookmarks** page, as shown above. Press and hold a bookmark icon to display the menu shown on the right, including options to edit and delete a bookmark.

| Open in new tab |
| Open in Incognito tab |
| Edit bookmark |
| Delete bookmark |

Displaying Your Browsing History

Google Chrome keeps a record, in chronological order, of all the web pages you've recently visited. Surprisingly there isn't a button to display the History feature. However it can easily be displayed by typing **chrome://history** into the search bar.

When you tap the Go key on the on-screen keyboard, as shown on the right, your **History** list is displayed, as shown below.

To save time when opening your History list, instead of entering **Chrome://history** into the search bar, create a **History** bookmark, as shown on the right and on page 79. Creating a bookmark is described on page 79. There are options on the History page to **CLEAR BROWSING DATA...** and **Search history**.

Communication and Social Networking

Introduction

This chapter describes the various ways a Nexus 9 tablet can be used to communicate with other people. Some of the main apps used for these activities are:

Gmail

Google e-mail used by businesses, friends and families to send messages, documents and photos all over the world.

Skype

Free worldwide *voice* and *video* calls between computers.

Facebook

The most popular *social networking* website. Enter your personal *profile* and *timeline* and make *online friends* with people having similar backgrounds and interests.

Twitter

Another very popular social networking site, based on short text messages (*140 characters maximum*) which can be read by anyone who chooses to follow the originator, who may be a celebrity, company or a member of the public.

LinkedIn

This is a special network used by professionals for developing their careers and exploring business opportunities, but is beyond the scope of this book.

Electronic Mail

Gmail is Google's electronic mail service. It's currently the most popular, ahead of other well-known services such as Microsoft's Outlook.com and Yahoo! Mail.

Gmail

Gmail is used for creating, sending and receiving text messages over the Internet. *Replies* can easily be sent to the original sender of a message you've received and, if necessary, to all other recipients of the original message. An e-mail can be *forwarded* to anyone else you think may be interested.

You can maintain an *address book* for all your contacts and *import* into it files of contacts from other e-mail services.

An e-mail message can include photos and documents, known as *attachments,* "clipped" to the message and sent with it.

Gmail is a web-based e-mail service, so you can access your electronic correspondence from anywhere in the world. All you need is a connection to the Internet and your Gmail username and password, as discussed on page 16. If someone has already used your chosen e-mail address, just add some numbers, such as **stellaaustin86@gmail.com**, to create a unique address.

There are two e-mail icons on the All Apps screen, the yellow **Email** app and the **Gmail** app shown above on the right. The Gmail app gives you access to Gmail and any other e-mail services you use, so you don't need to use the yellow **Email** icon. After tapping the Gmail icon, tap the 3-bar menu button and select the e-mail account you wish to use, as shown on the right.

Creating a Message

Tap the 3-bar menu button at the top left of the screen, shown on the previous page, then tap the **Compose** icon at the bottom right of the screen, shown here on the right.

The **Compose** screen opens, as shown below. Enter the main recipient's e-mail address in the **To** bar. Tapping the small arrow on the far right of **To** below opens two new lines for recipients who will receive either Carbon copies (**Cc)** or Blind carbon copies (**Bcc**). The latter don't know who else has received a copy.

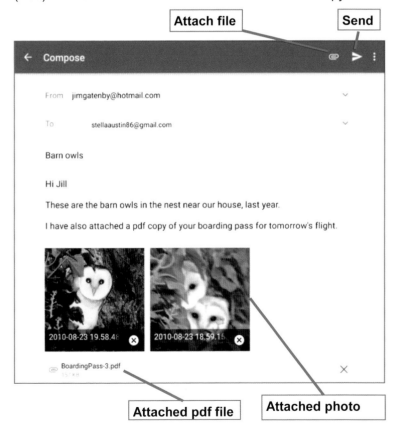

Adding an Attachment

Tap the **Attach file** icon shown on the right and on the
bar across the **Compose** screen on the previous page.
Then choose the location from which to select the photo
or document, etc., to attach to the message. Tap the required
photo, etc., and the attachment should appear on the e-mail, as
shown on the previous page. The attachments in this example
are the owls photos and a PDF document called **BoardingPass**.

Sending an E-mail

When you've finished composing the e-mail, tap the
Send button on the bar across the top of the **Compose**
screen, as shown on the right.

Receiving an E-mail

The e-mail will be available for reading by the recipient almost
immediately, or as soon as they open their *Inbox*. They will see
the sender's name and the text and photos as shown on the
previous page. Tapping a photo enlarges it fully on the screen.

To open an attached document, tap
its name or the paperclip icon, as
shown on the right. Tap the star icon
on the right and above to mark the e-mail as a *favourite*.
Icons at the top and bottom of the **Inbox** screen allow
you to reply to the sender, reply to all recipients of the original
message or forward the e-mail to someone else.

Skype

This is a service which allows you to make *voice* and *video* calls all over the world. Calls between two computers are absolutely free. If you use your tablet to call a mobile phone or landline there is a charge, for which you need a Skype account with some credit in it.

Hundreds of millions of people use Skype to make voice and video calls. You can also send photographs and instant text messages or make and send a video. Nexus 9 tablets are fully equipped for Skype, with a front-facing webcam and built in microphone and speakers. The rear-facing camera can be used to show views of your surroundings during a video call. The Skype app in the Google Play Store is free and, if necessary, can be installed as described in Chapter 3.

Start Skype by tapping its icon on the All Apps screen, as shown on the right. Then sign in using an existing Skype username and password or a Microsoft account. Alternatively, create a new Skype account. When you sign in, contacts from your address book are displayed, as shown below.

Skype

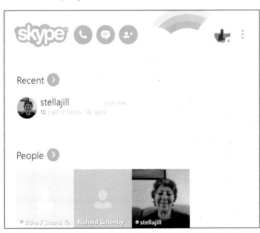

The Opening Skype Screen

Making a Skype Call

Any contacts currently online are displayed with a green dot, as shown on the right and at the bottom of the previous page.

Tap the name or thumbnail of a contact who is currently online. The following icons are available when making a Skype call:

    Start a voice only call

    Start a video call

When you call a contact, their photo and name appear on the screen. The functions of the icons are listed on the next page.

Making a Skype call

Receiving a Skype Call

When someone "Skypes" you, the tablet will emit a distinctive ring and the caller's name appears on the screen. Tap the green phone icon shown on the left below to answer the call.

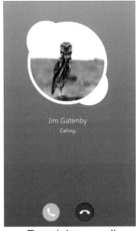

Receiving a call   Answering a call

Shown below are the main icons used when answering calls:

   Answer a video or voice call

   Switch video on or off

   Switch microphone on or off

  Show dialling pad and messages

  End or reject a call

Facebook

Facebook is the biggest social network, with over a billion users all over the world. To join Facebook, you must be aged over 13 years and have a valid e-mail address. You can access Facebook on a Nexus 9 using the Android Facebook app, if necessary installed from the Play Store, as discussed in Chapter 3. You also need to *sign up* for a Facebook account and in future *sign in* with your e-mail address and password.

Facebook

First you create your own *Profile* in the form of a *Timeline*, as shown on the right. This can include personal details such as your schools, employers and hobbies and interests. Facebook then provides lists of people with similar interests to yourself, who you may want to invite to be one of your Facebook *friends*. Anyone who accepts will be able to exchange news, information, photos and videos with you.

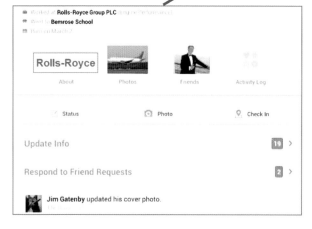

Facebook Security and Privacy

The *audience selector* shown on the right appears against the items of personal information in your profile. Tapping the audience selector displays a drop-down menu, as shown on the right, enabling you to set the level of privacy for each item, ranging from **Public** to **Only me**. **Public** means *everyone* can see the information, including people you don't know.

Status Updates

These are used to post your latest information and news and usually consist of a short text message and perhaps one or more photos. Tap **Status** on the centre left of the Facebook screen shown on the previous page to open the **Write Post** window shown below. Tap **To:** to select the audience. Then enter the text of your post, replacing **What's on your mind?** shown below.

Tap the camera icon at the bottom left of the screen to insert a photo from the internal storage of the tablet.

Finally tap **Post**, shown on the right above and your friends will receive the update in their *News Feed*.

Twitter

Like Facebook, Twitter is a social networking website used by hundreds of millions of people. There is a free app for Twitter in the Google Play Store. If necessary, the app can be installed as discussed in Chapter 3. Signing up to Twitter is free. Once signed

Twitter

up you can either use your e-mail address and password to sign in or you can enter your Twitter username such as **@jimsmith**. Some of the main features of Twitter are:

- Twitter is a website used for posting text messages, known as *tweets*, of up to 140 characters in length.

- You can include a 160 character *personal profile* on your Twitter page.

- Photographs can be posted with a tweet.

- Twitter is based on people *following*, i.e. reading the tweets of other people, such as celebrities, politicians and companies marketing their products or services.

- You can follow anyone you like, but you can't choose who follows you. If you have no followers, anything you post on Twitter will remain unread. You could encourage your friends and family to follow you and each other on Twitter, to share your latest news.

- *Hashtags*, such as *#climatechange*, for example, make it simple for other people to find all the tweets on a particular subject. The hashtag is included within a tweet. Tapping the hashtag displays all the tweets on that subject, which might be a campaign or a debate.

- If you like a tweet, it can be *retweeted* to all of your followers, together with comments of your own.

- You can send *replies* to a tweet.

Sending a Tweet

Tap **What's happening?** at the bottom left of the Twitter Home screen and then start typing your message.

The number **36** at the top right above is the number of characters still available to be used, out of the maximum of 140 allowed.

Two icons appear at the bottom of the **Tweet** window, as shown below. Tapping the left-hand icon uses the Nexus 9's built-in GPS system to pin-point your current location and include this as a note in the Tweet.

Tapping the right-hand icon above displays the two icons shown here on the right. The camera icon is used to take photos with either of the Nexus 9's built-in cameras. The right-hand icon is

used to select a photo already saved on the Nexus 9. The picture is then included in the tweet. When the tweet is finished, tap the TWEET button, as shown at the top right of this page. Your followers will see your tweet on their Twitter Home screen, as shown on the next page.

Tap the 3-dot menu button at the top right of the screen, then tap

Settings and **General**. Tap to tick the box next to **Image previews** to display photos in a tweet. If the box is not ticked, a blue text link is displayed instead, as discussed on the next page.

Responding to a Tweet

If the reader taps a tweet, the following toolbar is displayed.

These icons enable you to respond to a tweet in various ways. Reading from left to right, they are:

Reply, **Retweet**, mark as **Favorite** and **Share** with other people.

Viewing Photographs

As discussed on the previous page, depending on the **Settings**, instead of a photo, the reader of a tweet may see a blue link embedded in the text, such as **pic.twitter.com/g43TrgzchM** shown below. This link is created by Twitter automatically .

James Gatenby @gingatenby   17m
The cat we adopted from the rescue centre is now much more confident and is out in the fields most days. pic.twitter.com/ g43TrgzchM

Tap the blue text link shown above to full open the photo on the screen, as shown below.

8

Working With Photos

Introduction

The Nexus 9 is an ideal platform for taking, viewing and sharing photographs and videos.

As listed on page 2, the Nexus 9 has a 1.6 megapixel front camera, facing the user. This can be used in video calls or for taking "selfies". There is also an 8 megapixel rear camera which can be used for general photography. Switching between cameras is discussed shortly.

Some methods of putting photos and videos on the Nexus 9 are:

- Taking a photo (or making a video) with one of the Nexus 9's two built-in cameras.

- Copying photos onto the Nexus 9 from an SD card, flash drive or digital camera.

- Copying photos from a smartphone to the Nexus 9 using a *Bluetooth* wireless connection.

- Copying photos that have been stored on a laptop or desktop computer, as discussed in Chapter 9.

- Downloading photos from Facebook, Twitter or e-mail, as discussed in Chapter 7.

- Copying or *syncing* photos to the Nexus 9 from other computers using cloud storage systems such as *Google Drive* and *Dropbox*, as discussed in Chapter 9.

The photos can then be shared by uploading to Dropbox or Google Drive as discussed in Chapter 9 or posted in e-mails, Facebook or Twitter, as discussed in Chapter 7.

Using the Nexus 9's Built-in Cameras

Tap the camera icon shown on the right, on the All Apps screen, Home screen or Favorites tray. It will probably launch the rear camera ready for you to take  an ordinary photograph. To make a video call, when using Skype for example, the front camera launches automatically showing your face.

Switching Between Front and Rear Cameras

Tap the **Camera** icon shown above then tap the 3-dot circular menu button shown on the right. Next tap one of the two icons shown on the right below to switch between front and rear cameras. The icon changes as shown, depending on which camera is currently selected.

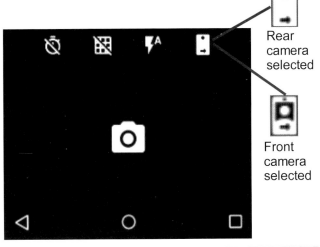

Rear camera selected

Front camera selected

Selecting Photo or Video Mode

Swipe in from the left and tap either **Camera** or **Video** from the menu on the left of the screen, shown here on the right.

Taking a Photo

Select **Camera** as shown on the previous page at the bottom right. Then tap the black and white **Camera** icon, shown here on the right, to take a photo with the selected camera. You will hear a noise as the photo is taken.

Making a Video

Select **Video** as shown on the previous page at the bottom right. Then tap the video camera icon shown on the right to start recording. Tap the square icon shown on the right to end the recording.

Viewing Photos and Videos

Thumbnails of the photos and videos taken with the Nexus 9 can now be viewed after tapping the **Photos** icon, shown on the right.

Tap to open a photo, then tap the 3-dot menu button shown on the right. This displays options including **Details**, **Print** and **Slideshow**.

Capturing a Screenshot

To capture a copy of the screen, simultaneously hold down the **Power** button and the **Volume** button (at the volume *down* end). The screenshot can then be viewed in the **Photos** app as described above, or sent using the sharing button shown below on the right. Shown on the right is a screenshot, as used in this book, of the Nexus 9 All Apps screen.

The *sharing* button shown on the right often appears and can be used to send a photo to Dropbox, Google Drive, e-mail, Facebook and Twitter, etc., etc.

The Photos App

Tap the **Photos** app on the Home or All Apps screen or on the Favorites bar, then tap the 3-bar menu at the top left of the screen, shown here on the right. This opens a menu with options including  **Photos**, **Albums** or **Videos**. **Photos** displays thumbnails of all your photos in the clouds or on the Nexus 9's internal storage. This includes photos taken with the in-built Nexus 9 cameras and also any photos you import from other devices such as SD cards and separate cameras. Shown below is a sample from the **Albums** option in **Photos**. These were imported from SD cards as discussed shortly.

Tap on a thumbnail to display a larger version of the photo.

Managing and Editing Photos

Open the **Photos** app as described on the previous page and then tap the image you wish to manage. Tap the 3-dot button on the top right of the screen to open a menu which includes options to **Print**, **Copy to album** or display a **Slideshow**.

On the lower right of the screen is an *auto enhance* icon, shown here on the right. Along the bottom of the **Photos** screen shown on the right is a toolbar, shown again below.

The pencil icon shown on the right and on the left above displays the editing toolbar shown below, with tools to auto enhance, crop, rotate and fine tune the image.

The dustbin icon shown on the right and on the upper toolbar above is used to delete the selected photo.

The sharing icon shown on the right allows you to send a copy of the photo to numerous destinations such as Gmail, Dropbox, Google Drive, Facebook, Twitter, etc., etc. Dropbox and Google Drive are cloud storage systems, discussed in more detail in Chapter 9.

Dropbox

Drive

Using the Nexus 9's Micro USB Port

The *Micro USB* port built into the Nexus 9 and shown on page 12 can easily be converted to a full-size standard USB port using an OTG (On The Go) cable, as shown on page 113.

The OTG cable can be used for connecting the following USB devices to the Nexus 9, for the importing of files such as photos.

- A standard SD card in a USB card reader.
- A USB flash drive/memory stick.
- A separate digital camera.

Connecting USB devices to the Nexus 9 is discussed in the Appendix.

Importing Photos from a USB Device

The Nexus Media Importer app is free and can be downloaded and installed from the Play Store as discussed in Chapter 3. Connect the USB device to the Nexus 9 using the OTG cable. The device is detected and in response to **Choose an app for the USB device**, tap **Nexus Media Importer**. Then tap **OK**, as shown below, to allow the Nexus Media Importer to access the USB device.

1. Nexus Media Importer
Homesoft
★ ★ ★ ★ ♪

Nexus Media Importer

Allow the app Nexus Media Importer to access the USB device?

☐ Use by default for this USB device

CANCEL   OK

Tap **All Photos** or **Folders** to open thumbnails of the photos on the device, as shown at the top of the next page.

All Photos   Folders

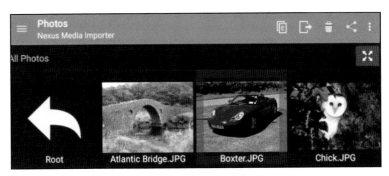

Viewing Photos Stored on an SD Card, etc.

To view a large version of photo on the SD card or flash drive, double tap a thumbnail, as shown above. You may wish to keep your photo collection on separate SD cards and always view them from the storage medium in this way.

Copying Photos to the Internal Storage

If you wish to save copies of photos on the internal storage of the Nexus 9, tap a thumbnail to display the tool icons shown below and on the top right above.

 Saves a **Copy** of the photo on the internal storage of the Nexus 9 in the **Pictures** folder, discussed shortly.

 The **Move** button *saves* a photo in the **Pictures** folder on the internal storage and deletes the original image from the SD card, or flash drive, etc.

 The **Delete** button removes photos from a USB storage medium such as an SD card or flash drive, etc.

 Use the **Share** button to send copies of photos to e-mail, **Photos**, Facebook, Twitter, Dropbox, Google Drive, etc.

 This **Menu** button has options including **Edit**, **Slide Show** and **Rotate,** etc.

Images sent to the **Photos** app, etc., using **Share** above are stored in the "clouds" as discussed in more detail in Chapter 9.

Viewing Photos on the Internal Storage

As stated on the previous page, you can save photos in the **Pictures** folder in the internal storage of the Nexus 9 by copying or moving them. To view the photos tap the **Photos** icon on the Home or All Apps screen as shown on the right.

Then tap the 3-bar menu icon on the top left of the **Photos** screen, as shown on the right.

From the drop-down menu which appears, tap **On device** to open the screen shown below.

As discussed on pages 96 and 97, the thumbnails can be enlarged by double tapping. You can also display options to **Edit**, **Share** and **Delete** photos after single tapping the thumbnail.

Photos on the Nexus 9 can also be viewed in the File Explorer feature on a Windows PC computer. Connect the Nexus 9 to a USB port on a PC using the Nexus 9 battery charger cable. On the PC computer, the Nexus 9 **Pictures** folder appears as:

Copying Photos from a Smartphone

This is done using the Nexus 9 and a phone with *Bluetooth* wireless technology built in. First the two devices must be *paired* i.e. connected wirelessly.

Pairing the Nexus 9 with a Smartphone

- In **Settings** on both devices, make sure Bluetooth is **On** and each device is set as **Discoverable** or **Visible to all Bluetooth devices nearby**.

- The phone should be detected and listed on the Nexus 9 under **Available devices.** Tap the name of the phone.

- Confirm that the same **PIN** number appears on both the Nexus 9 and the phone (a Blackberry in this example).

- The two devices are now *paired*, as shown below.

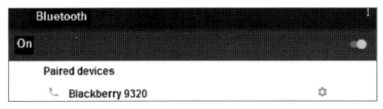

Transferring a Photo from the Smartphone to the Nexus 9

- Open the photo full-size on the smartphone.

- From the phone menu, select **Send** then **Bluetooth**.

- On the phone select **Nexus 9** under **Select Device.**

- The file transfer starts.

- On the Nexus 9, swipe down from the top to open the **Notifications** and tap **Do you want to receive this file?** and then tap **Accept** under **Accept the file?**

- The file transfer is completed and the file can now be viewed on the Nexus 9. Tap the **Photos** icon, then tap the 3-bar menu and select **On device**, as discussed at the top of page 100.

Google+ Auto-Backup

The Auto-Backup feature saves copies of your photos and videos to the clouds, including those you take with the internal cameras on the Nexus 9 and those you download from other sources.

To check that **Auto-Backup** is **On**, tap the **Photos** icon, then tap the 3-dot menu button. Next tap **Settings** then **Auto-Backup**. If necessary, tap the button to switch **Auto-backup On**, indicated by a blue button as shown below on the right.

Images listed in **On device** in **Photos**, discussed on page 99, may not be backed up automatically but this facility can be switched on using the cloud icon shown below on the right.

Select **On device** in **Photos**, as discussed on page 100. Against any group of photos such as **Pictures** shown below, there is a cloud icon. If the cloud has a line through it, tap the icon. The cloud changes to blue, as shown on the right, indicating that **Auto-Backup** is **On** for the **Pictures** folder.

With the blue cloud indicating that auto-backup is **ON**, all the photos you import will be backed up to the clouds. The new photos will now appear in **Photos** as well as **Photos/On device**.

To see the backed up photos type **#autobackup** in the **Photos** search bar, as shown below.

9

Cloud Computing and File Management

Introduction

Cloud computing is the storage of *files* such as photos and documents on powerful Internet computers known as *servers*. The servers are provided and managed by large companies such as Google and Dropbox. Storing many of your files in the clouds means you don't need bulky hard disc drives inside computers. This has contributed to the development of very small hand-held tablets like the Nexus 9, which can be just as powerful as much larger computers.

The general method is that you have a cloud storage app such as Google Drive or Dropbox. Dropbox provides up to 2GB of free storage space while more is available for a monthly fee. Google offers 15GB of free storage for Drive, Gmail and Google+ Photos. Apps for Dropbox and Drive can be downloaded from the Play Store if not already installed on the Nexus 9. The Dropbox or Google Drive app must be set up on each computer and you access it with a username and password.

When you save a file in, say, Dropbox, on one computer, it's automatically copied to the clouds and *synced* to all your other machines. For example, I use a desktop computer for typesetting the chapters of books such as this one. By saving each chapter in Dropbox on my desktop computer it's automatically synced to my other computers, including the Nexus 9. The Nexus 9 can open the chapters, which are saved as PDF (Portable Document Format) files. So I can read through and check the chapters anywhere at any time on the Nexus 9 or any other Internet computer.

Accessing Files in the Clouds

The very popular cloud storage apps, Dropbox and Google Drive are shown below in the Play Store. These may be already present on your Nexus 9 but, if not, they can be downloaded for free from the Play Store and installed as described in Chapter 3.

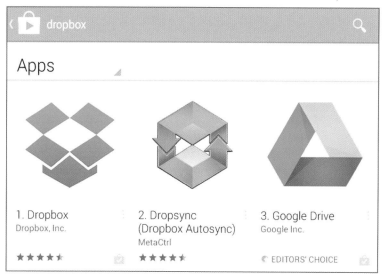

Dropbox

After you install Dropbox, create an account on the Nexus 9 by signing up with your e-mail address and password. If you have other computers such as a laptop or a desktop you can sign up to Dropbox on them as well after opening the website at:

www.dropbox.com

On a Windows PC machine this will place a **Dropbox** folder on the File Explorer, as shown on the right. Files you save in the Dropbox folder on the PC will be synced to Dropbox on your other computers such as the Nexus 9.

Similarly photos and other files saved on the Nexus 9 can be transferred to your other computers using the ***share*** icon on the

Nexus 9, shown on the left. This appears after opening the photo on the full screen and tapping it, as discussed on page 97.

This opens a window containing icons for lots of share destinations including Facebook, Twitter, Gmail, Google Drive and Dropbox. The icons for Drive and Dropbox are shown below.

Drive   Dropbox

Tap either of the icons shown above to copy the photo to Dropbox or Google Drive. (Drive is discussed on the next page). Files saved to Dropbox and Drive have several advantages:

- Files can be viewed on any computer connected to the Internet anywhere, once you've signed in to Dropbox.

- All computers have the same, latest versions of files.

- The files are professionally backed up and managed on the host server computers in the "clouds".

One risk is that if you accidentally delete a file on one machine, it will no longer be available on any of your other computers.

Cloud storage systems like Dropbox and Google Drive are extremely useful and efficient. However, it's also a good idea to make backup copies of important files on a separate storage medium such as a flash drive/memory stick.

Google Drive

Drive is Google's popular cloud storage system and, if not already present, can be installed from the Play Store, as described in Chapter 3.

Google Drive works in a very similar way to **Dropbox**, just described. You install the app on the Nexus 9 with a Gmail address and a password. The method of uploading files to **Drive** on the Nexus 9 is the same as sharing files to **Dropbox**, as just discussed on page 105.

On any other computers which you may use, install the app or, on laptop and desktop PCs, install a **Google Drive** folder, after visiting the website at www.drive.google.com. Next tap **Install Drive for your computer**. Repeat this for all the computers you wish to automatically sync files to.

Any files you *share* with **Drive** on the Nexus 9, will appear in **Drive** on all your other computers. Similarly, if you *drag and drop* files to the **Google Drive** folder on a laptop or desktop PC, as shown on the right, these files will automatically be synced to **My Drive** on the Nexus 9, as shown below. To display **My Drive** on the Nexus 9, tap the **Drive** icon shown at the top right of this page.

Google Docs

Once you've installed Google Drive you immediately have access to *Google Docs*, which is a suite of free *web-based software* and includes word processing and spreadsheet apps. This software is available on any computer with Google Drive installed, after you've signed in with your Gmail username and password.

Tap the **Drive** icon shown on the right to open **My Drive**, shown at the bottom of the previous page.

Scroll up through any documents and photos that you have saved in **My Drive**. At the bottom of the **My Drive** screen you should see the **New** document icon as shown on the right. Tap this icon to open the **New** document window shown below.

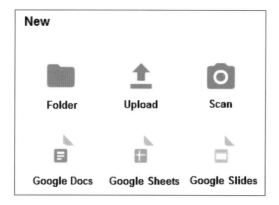

As shown above, the **New** window has apps to create various documents. Although **Google Docs** is the collective name for all the apps, it's also the name of the word processor app. Apart from the spreadsheet app, **Google Sheets**, there is **Google Slides** for preparing presentations and **Scan** which creates a scanned image of an object or document *PDF* file (Portable Document Format). You can also create your own folders.

Google Docs can also be opened by tapping the **Create** icon installed on the Nexus 9 Home screen by default, as shown on the right. As shown below, the **Create** window which opens has several of the apps which appear on the **New** window shown on the previous page. In addition, the **Keep** app shown below can be used as a notepad to keep personal notes, lists, reminders and photos, etc.

If, for any reason you can't find the **Create** app on your Home screen, you can obtain Google Docs, Sheets, Slides, Keep and Drive from the Play Store and install them, as discussed in Chapter 3. Then you can put the icons for the individual apps in your own **Create** folder on your Home screen, as discussed on page 28.

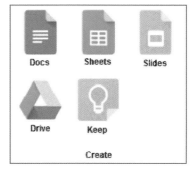

Using the Nexus 9 Like a Laptop

As discussed elsewhere in this book, you can buy a Google keyboard for the Nexus 9, which also acts as a cover. As discussed in the Appendix and elsewhere you can also connect the Nexus 9 to various USB and Bluetooth keyboards and mice. The Google Chromecast dongle plugs into an HDMI TV or monitor and allows the Nexus 9 screen to be "cast" to a large screen for increased productivity.

The spreadsheet, word processing and slide apps in Google Docs are free with Google Drive and easy to use. However the Docs apps have all the usual features needed to produce professional documents. They are also compatible with Google Docs used on PCs and Macs, making working on the same documents on different machines a straightforward process.

The Google Docs Word Processor

Tap the **Docs** icon shown on the previous page. The word processing screen opens ready for you to type a document.

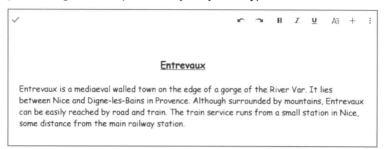

Double tap a word to select it for formatting. Further drop-down options are available from the menu bar across the top, including size, styles and colours of text and rename, print and **Keep on device**, i.e. save on the internal storage for off-line use.

When you've finished the document tap the tick in the left-hand corner and the document is saved to Google Drive. It can now be viewed on any other computer where you are signed in to Drive.

The Google Docs Spreadsheet

Tap the **Sheets** icon shown on the previous page to open the spreadsheet. As shown below, **Sheets** has all the usual tools for creating and formatting a spreadsheet.

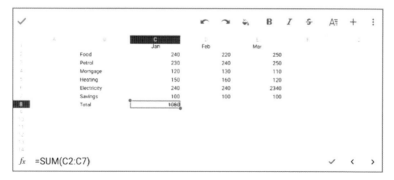

Making Files in the Clouds Viewable Offline

You may need to view photos and other files offline, where you have no Wi-Fi. You can check a file for offline access by turning Wi-Fi Off, as discussed on page 15, then trying to open the file.

Offline Access in Dropbox

Open the listing of files and photos in Dropbox then tap the circled down arrow. Now tap the **Favorite** star to make the file viewable offline. Alternatively open the file fully on the screen and tap the **Favorite** star at the top right.

Offline Access in Google Drive

Open the file or file listing in Drive and tap the icon shown on the right. Then make sure **Keep on device** is switched On as shown by the green button below.

To view the files available offline, tap the 3-bar menu icon in Google Drive, shown on the right, then tap **On device**.

File Management Using a PC

You can use a laptop or desktop PC computer to manage the files on a Nexus 9. Connect the Nexus 9 to a USB port on the laptop or desktop machine, using the cable supplied to charge the Nexus 9's battery. The Internal Storage of the Nexus 9 appears in the File Explorer on the PC just like an external disc drive or flash drive, etc.

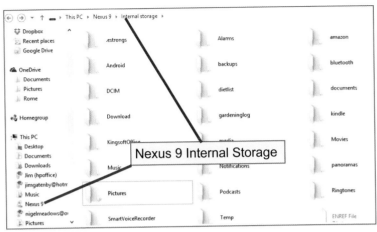

Nexus 9 Internal Storage

Nexus 9 folders viewed in File Explorer on a PC

Connecting the Nexus 9 to a PC enables the full range of File Explorer or Windows Explorer tools to be applied to the Nexus 9 folders. You can see the folders that are stored on the Nexus 9 such as **Pictures** and **Bluetooth** as shown above.

You can also create new folders on the Nexus 9 and move files to different folders by dragging and dropping or cutting and pasting. Right-clicking a Nexus 9 folder opens a menu including the options shown on the right. While the Nexus 9 is connected to a PC, you can also connect flash drives and SD cards, etc. to the PC. This allows the PC to be used to transfer files between the Nexus 9 and the flash drives and other external storage media.

File Manager Apps for the Nexus 9

Several free file manager apps are available from the Play Store, such as ES File Explorer and File Manager. Apps such as WPS Office (also known as Kingsoft Office) can be used on the Nexus 9 to open documents created on a PC in formats such as .doc, .docx, .txt, .pdf, .xls, .xlsx and .csv.

Cloud Printing from the Nexus 9

Google Cloud Print is a free app used for printing from a tablet like the Nexus 9 and installed from the Play Store as described in Chapter 3.

Cloud Print

If you have a printer connected by a cable to a laptop or desktop PC, this is referred to as a *Classic* printer and needs to be set up in the Google Chrome Web browser as described below. (A *Cloud Ready* wireless printer connects to the Web without being attached to a computer. This shouldn't need any setting up).

For setting up, a classic printer is attached to a laptop or desktop computer which has Chrome installed. Open Chrome on the PC and make sure you're signed in with your Gmail address and password. Open the Chrome menu by clicking the icon shown on the right.

From the menu, select **Settings** and then scroll down the screen and at the bottom select Show advanced settings. Scroll down the next screen and under **Google Cloud Print** select **Manage** and then **Add printers**. Select the printer you wish to use, as shown below. Then tap **Add printer** to complete the process.

Google cloud print
beta

Printers to register

Google Cloud Print has detected the following printers connected to your computer. Click below to add the selected printers to Google Cloud Print for account jimgatenby59@gmail.com

This step is not required to print to Google Cloud Print. Clicking "Add printer(s)" will just add your local printers to your account. Cloud Ready Printers can connect directly without this step.

✓   EPSON XP-312 313 315 Series

To print an image in **Photos**, open the photo full size and tap the 3-dot menu button and tap **Print**. Select your printer after tapping in the top left-hand corner of the screen and finally tap the Cloud Print icon shown on the upper right. To print a document in Google Docs, tap the middle icon shown on the right, then tap the **Print** icon, which appears as shown here on the bottom right.

Appendix: Useful Accessories

The Nexus 9 is a complete computer in itself, capable of executing a vast range of tasks. However, there may be occasions when you want to expand the basic tablet by connecting external devices, such as:

- A separate *keyboard* and *mouse*, so that you can use the Nexus 9 more like a laptop.
- A *digital camera* for viewing and transferring photos .
- An *SD card reader* for transferring photos and other files and adding to the internal storage of the Nexus 9.
- A *flash drive*, also known as a *memory stick* for transferring photos and other files.
- A *Chromecast dongle* which allows you view the display from the Nexus 9 on an HDMI TV screen.

Connecting USB (Universal Serial Bus) Devices

USB ports or sockets are a common way of connecting peripheral devices like keyboards. The Nexus 9 has a Micro USB port as shown on page 12. This can be converted to a full-size standard USB port using an *OTG* (*On The Go*) cable, as shown below.

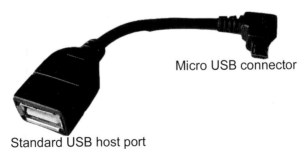

Micro USB connector

Standard USB host port

An OTG Cable

Simply plug the Micro USB connector on the OTG cable into the Micro USB port at the bottom of the Nexus 9. Connect the cable on the USB keyboard or mouse, etc., to the standard USB host port on the OTG cable, as shown on the previous page.

Connecting Several USB Devices

If you wish to connect a USB keyboard and a mouse simultaneously, you can use a multi-port *USB hub*, as shown below. This plugs into the standard USB host port on the OTG cable and provides several standard USB ports for accessories such as a USB keyboard, mouse, SD card reader and flash drive.

Multi-port USB hub

USB SD Card Reader

The SD card reader shown on the right is inserted directly into the USB host port on the OTG cable. The SD card can be used to transfer photos from a camera to the Nexus 9. Then they can be viewed, edited and saved in various locations including the "clouds" on the Internet, as discussed in Chapters 8 and 9. The SD card can also be used as extra storage.

USB card reader
and SD card

Flash Drive

A USB flash drive can be used for importing photos, etc., to the Nexus 9 in a similar way to the card reader above.

A digital camera can be connected using the camera's USB battery charger cable.

USB flash drive

USB (Universal Serial Bus) devices like keyboards, mice, and flash drives are inexpensive and are *plug and play* — they work straightaway as soon as they are connected.

Wireless Keyboard and Mouse

A *wireless receiver dongle* (similar in appearance to a flash drive) plugs into the USB host port on the OTG cable shown on page 113. The keyboard and mouse should work straightaway.

Bluetooth

This is a technology for connecting devices wirelessly over short distances. The Nexus 9 has Bluetooth technology built in. This allows the Nexus 9 to be connected or *paired* with compatible accessories, such as Bluetooth keyboards and mice.

Pairing a Bluetooth Device with the Nexus 9

If necessary, switch On the device such as a keyboard, mouse or phone, etc., and on a phone make sure Bluetooth is also On. On the Nexus 9 swipe down from the top and tap the **Settings** icon on the Quick Start panel, shown on the right and on page 16. Switch Bluetooth On by tapping the solid circle shown in green below on the right.

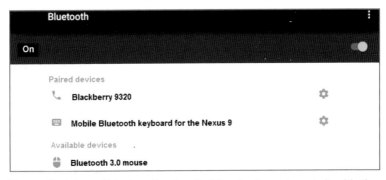

Tap a device as listed under **Available devices** to pair it with the Nexus 9. You may be asked to enter a pin number or check that the same number appears on both devices. **Paired devices** shown above have a wireless connection to the Nexus 9. For example, you could copy a photo from the Blackberry phone to the Nexus 9, as discussed in Chapter 8, or use the Bluetooth keyboard to type on the Nexus 9 screen.

Chromecast

As shown on the right, the Chromecast is a thumb-sized *dongle* which plugs into an HDMI port on an HDMI television. This enables videos, web pages, music, photos etc., on the Nexus 9 to be simultaneously viewed on a large screen.

Chromecast

The basic setting up procedure is as follows:

- Insert the Chromecast into the HDMI port on the TV.

- Set the input source on the TV to HDMI.

- Connect the Chromecast to a wall socket using the power cable provided with the Chromecast.

- On the Nexus 9, download the Chromecast app from the Play Store, as discussed on page 33 and 34.

Chromecast

- Use the Chromecast app to connect the Chromecast device to your wireless network, using your router password and giving a name to your Chromecast dongle.

- Open a video, etc., on the Nexus 9. The Cast button shown on the right should appear on the top right of the screen, as shown below. If you can't see the Cast button, try restarting the router.

- Tap the Cast button to start mirroring the Nexus 9 screen to the TV via your wireless router.

Another way to start casting is to tap the Chromecast icon on the Quick Settings panel, as shown on the right and on page 45.

Cast screen

Chromecast can be used to display web pages, photos, Play Music, NETFLIX and YouTube videos. A more complete list of apps which are compatible with Chromecast can be found at:-

www.chromecast.com/apps

Index

117